wild MOCKTAILS
AND HEALTHY COCKTAILS

Wild MOCKTAILS
AND HEALTHY COCKTAILS
HOME-GROWN AND FORAGED LOW-SUGAR RECIPES
from the MIDNIGHT APOTHECARY

LOTTIE MUIR

CICO BOOKS
LONDON NEW YORK

For my co-adventurer and partner EJ, who continues to share the chaos, cocktails, and cock-ups with (usually) unfailing good humor and love.

Published in 2018 by CICO Books
An imprint of Ryland Peters & Small Ltd
20–21 Jockey's Fields   341 E 116th St
London WC1R 4BW   New York, NY 10029

www.rylandpeters.com

10 9 8 7 6 5 4 3 2 1

A CIP catalog record for this book is available from the Library of Congress and the British Library.

ISBN: 978 1 78249 443 0

Printed in China

Editor: Caroline West
Designer: Geoff Borin
Photographer: Kim Lightbody, plus see page 176 for additional credits
Author photograph: Ashley Bradley

In-house editor: Dawn Bates
Art director: Sally Powell
Production manager: Gordana Simakovic
Publishing manager: Penny Craig
Publisher: Cindy Richards

Foraging wild ingredients requires expert knowledge and identification. The photographs and text in this book should not be used alone for identification purposes. The author and publisher cannot be held responsible for, nor shall be liable for, the erroneous consumption of wild plants that have caused severe or allergic reactions resulting from misidentification, nor the overconsumption of wild plants that have been shown to be toxic when consumed in large doses.

CONTENTS

FOREWORD

Lottie Muir's second book *Wild Mocktails and Healthy Cocktails* from the Midnight Apothecary is a fascinating and exciting addition to her earlier book *Wild Cocktails*. This book takes you on a journey from the hedgerow to the kitchen garden, from alcoholic infusions to cultured drinks, and, on the way, devotes a wonderful chapter to plants with health benefits.

Lottie not only covers how to make wild mocktails and cocktails from foraged ingredients, but also health-giving drinks such as spring tonics and kombucha. I particularly loved her tea-based cocktails, which can make wonderful cold spritzers for a hot summer's evening that tantalize all the senses. Her transformation from student of the year at Capel Manor to the Midnight Apothecary and the toast of London in five years, illustrates how Lottie has combined her knowledge of both garden and foraged plants with the pleasure of creating a taste explosion.

Throughout the book there are clear instructions on what to harvest, where to harvest, and what equipment you will need. Lottie also offers advice on what is new in the cocktail cabinet, such as healthy sweeteners, miracle berries, and aquafaba. There are alcoholic infusions, cordials and syrups, bitters and instant sodas, as well as delicious recipes such as the Wild Negroni for real cocktail connoisseurs.

I find Lottie's zest for taste, texture, and flavor fascinating and very inspiring. I cannot wait to try the Quince Vodka with Szechuan Pepper, Star Anise, and Juniper Berries. Even typing this combination of flavors makes my mouth water with anticipation. Equally, being a vermouth fan, I am fascinated by her Wild Dry Vermouth. Lottie's great skill in this book lies in the combinations of flavors which, personally, I would never have dreamt of. It is the daring and the unexpected that make this book come alive...

Jekka McVicar

INTRODUCTION

My first book *Wild Cocktails* was all about maximizing flavor and balance in plant-centered, (mainly) boozy, and (occasionally) non-boozy concoctions by whatever edible and legal means necessary. Using botanical ingredients grown at home, whether foraged close by or found at the local market, the pleasure principle was very much to the fore. While the book looked at the restorative and medicinal aspects of plants—and scored a few "low-carbon footprint" points for seasonality and locality—if it took a lot of sugar to get a balanced cocktail, I didn't balk. I still think the recipes are pretty delicious, if I say so myself, but things, and I, have moved on a bit.

raspberry

Don't worry. The drinks in this new book—whether alcoholic or not—will be luxurious and to be enjoyed, not endured. But if the line between cocktails and healthy diets is becoming increasingly blurred, I'd say we're onto a winner.

The desire to cut out, or at least severely reduce, refined sugar in our diets continues to grow. It's true that most of the sugar we consume, regardless of whether it's refined white sugar or a natural sweetener such as fruit or honey, will end up as glucose or fructose in our body at some point. And in excess that's not good. (I've had some fun finding a few exceptions, which I am excited to share with you later in the book.) But the point for me, and possibly for you, is to reduce sugar consumption in general and especially that of refined, heavily processed sweeteners that are harmful to us and the environment.

Although you may be cutting out sugar, you are also adding a wealth of nutrients, taste, and good looks to your drinks in the form of plants. These plants can be grown or foraged by you at minimal cost and with maximum enjoyment and health benefits. I have included a chapter on a few plant stars that score high on all three counts: taste, good looks, and health benefits.

The choice to consume no alcohol is also becoming more common, whether for health or religious reasons. Shortly after I made the semi-virtuous decision to include more mocktails and much less sugar in my diet, as well as in the menu at Midnight Apothecary, I went to a cocktail bar in London that served only non-alcoholic cocktails. Hoping to find the Holy Grail, I found that, although the drinks were delicious, some were overwhelmingly sweet and others reminded me of what I have in the morning for a healthy breakfast. Or they simply lacked the mouth-feel and va va voom that I consider vital for a cocktail.

Regardless of health, our Western palates are moving away from sweet and fruity toward drier, more aromatic, and bitter-forward drinks. Aperitifs and amari in general have made a huge comeback, which reflects this, as well as a trend toward lower or no-alcohol serves. The trick is to dial down the sweetness, while still balancing the strong, bitter, sour, salt, and umami elements. This isn't straightforward. As with salt for a chef, "sugar" is still an important element in many drinks (including amari)—not just for its sweetness, but also for its mouth-feel and flavor-extracting and preserving properties.

This new healthy foray has led me to discover other ways to play with the taste buds—from getting them just as stimulated with bitter or umami, as opposed to sweet sensations, to giving a drink viscosity with oil and proteins such as egg white (or canned chickpea/garbanzo bean water), as opposed to sugar. From taste-tripping parties

flowering currant

or plants like sweet cicely or yacón fruit. Or I can go down the whole amari route and play around with bitterness and aromatics using natural sweeteners.

For many of us, the ethics surrounding our food and drink purchases are as important as our health choices. I don't want to consume coconut sugar as a healthy natural sweetener if it means a rainforest was razed to the ground to grow that particular brand. Or to have a natural sweetener flown from the other side of the world when I might get equally pleasing results from something growing near me, such as beets (beetroot) or yacón fruit. But what this means will obviously differ according to where you are reading this. If you're in California, for example, an organically produced raw agave syrup from Mexico is likely to have a lighter carbon footprint than if I were to buy it here in the U.K. And what I can buy here is more commonly a heavily chemically processed, fructose-packed version using the agave root, which doesn't do my health, pocket, or taste buds any good. So, this book is all about finding delicious, organic (when possible), ethically sourced ingredients that grow near you. If that's not always achievable, then hey, we can't always be saints.

What hasn't changed is the childlike pleasure to be gained from discovering ingredients that are literally growing all around you. Whether in your local street, park, hedgerow, or beach—or in your backyard or at a local farmers' market—these ingredients are about using amazing, organic, nutritious plants to give you enormous pleasure (and health benefits), as you get to know them intimately throughout the seasons and also through their lifecycles.

One of the most pleasurable aspects of creating this book has been inviting other foragers and gardeners to share a cocktail or mocktail recipe, using ingredients that are special to them. It has meant visiting them in their own particular paradise, hanging out with them, playing with them, and, most of all, learning from them. Each has a vast array of knowledge and experience that they have generously shared. What they all have in common is a desire to share their childlike wonder for the relationship we can enjoy with the plants growing among us—for their profound benefits to our bodies, our minds, and the land around us.

So I hope this book will be for you what it has been for me—an opportunity to recharge your palate, play with new plants, and get inventive in your desire for health and pleasure in a glass. Cheers!

using miracle berries (see page 19) to "adventures in mold" using kombucha, kefir, or kvass, the idea is to provide something grown-up, interesting, and delicious. Where I have needed an additional sweet element in a cocktail, I have found an abundance of natural organic sweeteners that do the job beautifully and can be used in much smaller quantities than refined sugar.

Lots of the ingredients from the last book haven't changed. It's more about changing your approach to what you do with them. So, whereas before I may have boiled up some herbs with a huge mound of refined sugar to make a syrup or added a massive dollop of sugar to them in some alcohol to make a liqueur, I have been more inclined to make an unsweetened tea. Or, as in my last book, I've used the properties of high-proof alcohol to do the job of extraction beautifully. From the unsweetened tea or alcohol (which already has a degree of sweetness), I can add further fresh aromatic or bitter herbs to the final drink and/or some type of water mixer and concentrated bitters that have further tiny elements of sweetness. With my unsweetened tea I can make a syrup with a tiny amount of natural sweetener such as maple syrup (which is a lot sweeter than sugar and therefore needed in smaller quantities); raw honey (which, although it contains sugar, is not refined and also has trace vitamins and minerals);

CHAPTER 1
THE NEW COCKTAIL CABINET

This book is all about making the most of beautiful, natural, and beneficial ingredients that are either growing close to you or can be sourced locally. There's a lot of noise and myth about the different "healthy sweeteners" on the market and I've had fun experimenting with many of them. I also consider some of the myths surrounding glucose and fructose—both simple sugars and both present in most natural ingredients, in spite of what advertisers may tell you—which you might be interested in. The sweeteners I've suggested you use are ones that may be growing close to you, contain no additives, have had little processing, and bring lots of added health benefits. I've also made suggestions for staple ingredients and other delights for your pantry, some basic equipment and techniques to get your cocktail hour going, and the most suitable glassware to use. Health and pleasure can be combined. Enjoy!

THE SKINNY ON THE SWEET

You may not consciously think of bitters, tonic water, or an innocent-looking strawberry as containing sugars but they are, of course, packed with them in different forms and quantities. Even wine and spirits, such as vodka and gin, have a tiny amount of fructose. However, just as salt and pepper are vital seasonings for a chef, so too is sweetness in some form essential for a cocktail-maker to balance bitter and herbal flavors.

We know refined sugar is bad for us, period. It is processed, bleached, lacks any nutrients, and, in excess, overloads our insulin-producing pancreas and liver to a point where neither can cope and serious health problems may ensue. Many people are now looking to replace refined sugar in their diets with "healthy sweeteners." However, there is a gray area surrounding what constitutes a healthy sweetener, which is prone to cynical marketing ploys and dubious ethics. With this in mind, I'd like to highlight the six key facts on which I've based my choice of sweeteners in this book:

• An element of sweetness is necessary in nearly every mocktail or cocktail.

• Most sugars, whether in plants and honey or in a refined processed state, contain a mix of glucose and fructose in differing proportions.

• Glucose is an essential molecule for life and, in a healthy diet, is very easily metabolized by the body to provide the energy we need to survive.

• Fructose, which is found naturally in fruit and honey, is easily digested in small quantities as part of a healthy diet. In large quantities, however, it puts a strain on the liver and can lead to major health problems.

• Highly processed sweeteners, even when they are based on nutrient-rich plants or honey, will lose their nutritional benefits if heated to a high temperature.

• Unprocessed sweeteners that have been flown thousands of miles around the world and/or grown on rainforest or pristine land razed to create that yield are unethical, even if they are packed with nutritional benefits.

In a healthy diet, in which the majority of the food intake is fresh, unprocessed food such as vegetables, fruit, nuts, seeds, and wholegrains (i.e. complex carbohydrates), every cell in the body is very happy to metabolize these starches and convert them into glucose to provide energy. Fructose (also found naturally in fruit, vegetables, and honey) can be converted too but, in contrast, only liver cells can break it down. This is fine in small quantities because the foodstuffs containing fructose also come with a host of beneficial vitamins, antioxidants, and fiber, and a healthy body has a fully functioning pancreas and liver to manage the process.

Difficulties arise because, in our processed-food culture, we have gone from consuming an average of ½oz (15g) of fructose per day in the early 1900s, mostly from fruit and vegetables, to nearly 2oz (55g) today. There has been a parallel rise in levels of obesity and diabetes, as well as the emergence of a new condition called non-alcoholic fatty liver disease. This is because one of the end products of processing fructose in the liver is triglyceride, a form of fat. Uric acid and free radicals are also formed. Triglycerides can damage liver function and contribute to a buildup of fatty plaques in the arteries. Free radicals can damage cell structures, enzymes, and even genes.

Uric acid can also turn off the production of nitric oxide, a substance that helps protect artery walls from damage. Another effect of a high-fructose intake is insulin resistance, which can be a precursor to diabetes.

However, it's not all bad news. History has taught us that moderation is key, our bodies are amazing, and plants are our allies. By relearning the medicinal benefits of the herbs known to our ancestors, we can enjoy a small amount of natural sugar and a lot of beneficial plant life in some delicious and healthy drinks!

There are a few basic rules of thumb if you wish to lower your sugar intake, stay healthy, and have a balanced and delicious drink. Where possible, use sparkling water in place of tonic waters, fruit juices, and other mixers. When deciding on the sweet element to use in a drink, opt for sweet ingredients that also have added health benefits.

There should be several local, sustainable sweet alternatives available to you that are both healthy and delicious in small quantities. These might include beets (beetroot), raw honey, dates, figs, grapes, sweet herbs (such as sweet cicely), bee pollen, pine pollen, and whole fruit packed with goodness.

A couple of pet peeves: Avoid using agave nectar, if possible. This is marketed as a "healthy sweetener" because it is high in fructose (up to 97 percent) and low on the glycemic index, but it is, in fact, no such thing. Fructose in small quantities as part of a healthy diet is fine, but it is only low on the glycemic index because it is processed in the liver. Finally, while the agave plant may have antioxidant and anti-inflammatory properties, the high-temperature processing and additions made to most commercial agave products remove those benefits. Even the inulin in fructose—a good source of fiber—is destroyed in the process.

On the other hand, raw coconut nectar (or coconut palm nectar) is meant to be healthy for the opposite reason: it is very low in fructose (about 10 percent) and produced at low temperatures to preserve its health-giving properties. Formed from the sweet sap tapped from flowering coconut blossom stems, it is organic, raw (so the enzymes are still active), and packed with amino acids and

almonds

quite a few vitamins and minerals. It may, however, have traveled long distances to reach you. Personally, I am uncomfortable with the sustainability of such crops and whether they need to be transported from the other side of the world when more local and equally healthy alternatives are available. But that's an environmental rather than a health concern. Others would argue coconut nectar is an environmentally friendly sweetener because it's claimed coconut palms produce 50 to 75 percent more sugar per acre than sugar cane. Despite this, I would still prefer to use something from closer to home.

maple leaf

HEALTHY ALTERNATIVES TO SUGAR

If you are looking to reduce the amount of refined sugar in your diet, then consider trying some of the healthy sweeteners available to you and use them instead of sugar in delicious drinks and in your diet in general.

BEE POLLEN

Bee pollen is incredibly sweet, makes an attractive rim on a drink, and has just about all the nutrient requirements needed by humans to survive. It is about 40 percent pollen and rich in vitamins, minerals, proteins, lipids and fatty acids, enzymes, carotenoids, and bioflavonoids. It has powerful antibacterial, antifungal, and antiviral properties that strengthen the capillaries, reduce inflammation, stimulate the immune system, and lower cholesterol levels naturally. Try using bee pollen in the Douglas Fir Gin and Bee Pollen Cocktail (see page 150).

BEETS

Beets (beetroot) are naturally sweet and packed with vitamins and minerals but, of course, they have their own flavor profile and make a drink opaque. They work wonderfully with earthy spirits but, if you want to make a drink more healthy and grown-up, why not ferment the beets to make a potent probiotic mixer for a non-alcoholic Regal Mary Mocktail (see page 148). Using raw cacao nibs with beets gives them a balanced bitterness, as well as sweetness—try them in the Beet, Cacao Nib, and Yacón Syrup Mocktail (see page 136).

BIRCH SAP

The natural sap from birch trees is mildly sweet, with the consistency of thin, syrupy water. It makes a beautiful, delicate mixer packed with vitamins and minerals, including vitamin C, potassium, manganese, thiamin, and calcium, and will also do wonders for your liver and kidneys. You can either collect your own sap (see How to Tap Birch Sap, on page 131) or buy it online or at health food stores. Keep fresh sap in your refrigerator or freezer, as it doesn't last beyond a few days. I like to use fresh sap in a number of drinks, including the Roast Quince, Szechuan Pepper, Juniper, and Star Anise Mocktail (see page 138). The sap can also be fermented and used in various drinks (see Fermented Birch Sap, on page 130).

KOMBUCHA

Kombucha fermentation breaks down sucrose into fructose and glucose, which feed the yeast that feeds the bacteria which feeds you. This produces a pleasantly sweet and very healthy drink that provides an excellent mixer or basis for a mocktail (see *Chapter 6: Cultured Drinks*, pages 118–33).

raw wildflower honey   *raw dark honey*   *brown rice syrup*   *coconut blossom nectar*

MOLASSES

Molasses is a by-product from the refining of raw sugar and goes through multiple boiling processes. The residue from the first boiling is known as light or mild molasses. The second boiling produces dark or full molasses.

Blackstrap molasses The result of a third and final boiling, this type of molasses is thicker than both light and dark molasses and also has a bitter flavor. Blackstrap molasses is classed as a nutritional supplement, as it contains minerals such as iron, calcium, and copper. It has complex notes of acidity, bitterness, and sweetness that pair well with brown spirits and autumnal fruits. The molasses needs diluting at a ratio of 1 part molasses to 1 part water, and a little goes a long way. I use it in a ginger bug for Homemade Ginger Ale (see page 132).

Grape, date, and pomegranate molasses These delicious sweeteners are the result of long reductions of grapes, dates, or pomegranates, but involve no refined sugar. They lend complex sweet, savory, acidic, and tart notes to a drink and provide the pleasant viscosity and texture of syrup. They take time and patience to make. For pomegranate molasses, 32oz (960ml) of pomegranate juice will reduce to a scant cup (250ml) of molasses in an hour over a low heat. For dates, add just enough water to a saucepan to cover, let boil, and reduce the heat to a simmer for 10 minutes. Then cool and blend or purée into a thick syrup. Grape molasses is prized for its high potassium and iron content. Simply boil down freshly pressed grape juice for about an hour, sieve, and then boil down again to about a tenth of the original volume. If you combine grape molasses, dates, and rose water, topped up

with some pine nuts or almonds and raisins, you'll have a delicious Middle Eastern thirst-quencher called Jallab.

RAISINS

Raisins are, of course, shriveled grapes and are very sweet. Adding them to birch sap provides an element of fermentation and sweetness (see Fermented Birch Sap, on page 130).

RAW HONEY

Raw honey (as opposed to pasteurized honey that's been heated) is loaded with antibacterial and antifungal properties, and may help with allergies if you use a local honey full of the pollen that affects you. Note that honey is loaded with fructose, so go steady with it. Honey is, however, sweeter than sugar, so you can use 25 percent less honey than refined sugar for the same sweetening effect. For this reason, you only need to use a tiny amount in water heated just enough to dissolve the honey without destroying its health-boosting properties (see Honey Syrup box, on page 16).

SWEET HERBS

A number of herbs, such as sweet cicely, angelica, and stevia, can be used to sweeten drinks. Sweet cicely (*Myrrhis odorata*) is an herbaceous perennial that makes a great natural sweetener. The strong, sweet, anise flavor of the leaves, seeds, and roots pairs well with rhubarb and gooseberries, but not so well with more delicate flavors. You can use chopped sweet cicely leaves to replace sugar in a drink recipe, but use with caution as they have a strong anise flavor. Try sweet cicely in the Roast Rhubarb,

date syrup   *grape molasses*   *yacón syrup*   *blackstrap molasses*

HONEY SYRUP

For a drink to have the maximum amount of flavor and least amount of sweetness it is preferable to first make the syrup using the full amount of recommended honey, to achieve the optimum level of flavor and mouth-feel, and then reduce the final amount of syrup used in the recipe. This is better than making weak and watery syrup and using more of it in volume. Heather Honey Syrup is simply syrup made with honey from bees that have gorged on the nectar and pollen of heather flowers.

Honey is usually too viscous to go straight into a drink, so needs to be diluted. I prefer a ratio of 2:1 honey to water to preserve its taste and mouth-feel. If you're using raw honey, DO NOT BOIL! This will kill all its antibacterial properties and any other nutrients. Simply warm the honey and water in a saucepan, stirring gently to dissolve the honey. As soon as the honey has dissolved, let cool slightly and funnel into sterilized bottles (see page 24). Refrigerate and consume within 2 weeks. If you add a tablespoon of 80-proof (40%-ABV) alcohol, you will increase the syrup's shelf life to a month.

Blood Orange, Sweet Cicely, and Lemongrass Mocktail (see page 139) and Wild Homemade Aquavit (see page 64). Both the leaves and stalks of *Angelica archangelica* (see page 28) taste sweet, again with an anise flavor, and can also be used as a natural sweetener with rhubarb and gooseberries.

Sugarleaf or sweetleaf (*Stevia rebaudiana*) is a perennial herb whose leaves have been used for hundreds of years as a natural sweetener because they are 250 to 300 times sweeter than natural sugar. Stevia was not recognized as a sweetener until 2008 in the USA and in 2011 in the European Union. It has an aniseed, almost bitter, aftertaste. You can find highly processed versions that don't taste as strongly of aniseed, but I prefer something less processed. The stevioside—the sweet element in the plant—differs greatly according to how much sun and warmth the plant has received, so use with caution. Stevia doesn't provide the same mouth-feel or consistency as sugar, but you can make a syrup by dissolving 1 part stevia to 3 parts water to use in mocktails or cocktails that already have a strong texture from fruit or dairy ingredients. Stevia can also be used in a hot-brew tea (see page 95).

SYRUPS

Licorice syrup Licorice (*Glycyrrhiza glabra*) is a natural root that has been used to flavor drinks and candy for a long time (for more on this plant, see page 30). There are two problems with licorice root. The first is that glycyrrhizin, the constituent that makes it sweet, is not for everyone—it shouldn't be used for those with high blood pressure. Secondly, licorice root, even if you peel, bash, and simmer it in water to make a basic licorice extract, is quite weak and not very sweet. So, I make Thyme and Licorice Syrup (see page 73) and add a bit of honey to give it the necessary va va voom!

Maple syrup For North American readers, this can be a locally sourced and utterly delicious sweetener made from boiling and reducing the sap of sugar maple (*Acer saccharum*) trees. It takes about 40 gallons (150 liters) of sap to produce 1 gallon (3.5 liters) of maple syrup. Maple syrup contains no chemical additives, preservatives, or agents—for more on the health benefits of this syrup, see page 37.

Yacón syrup Native to the Andes Mountains in South America and used for thousands of years (and one of the last crops of the Incas), the juice of the roots of the yacón plant (*Smallanthus sonchifolius*) is extracted, filtered, and evaporated in a chemical-free, very natural manufacturing process, similar to that of maple syrup. The resulting syrup has the consistency of molasses and a sweet pleasant taste that hints at caramel-y apple or pear. The exciting thing about yacón is that it contains sugar molecules (fructooligosaccharides), which are unrecognizable to the human digestive system, and so aren't digested. In addition, these fructooligosaccharides are very beneficial to our gut health, as they are prebiotics that feed the friendly bacteria in our intestines. They are also a source of soluble fiber. Try using yacón syrup in the Beet, Cacao Nib, and Yacón Syrup Mocktail (see page 136).

WHOLE FRUIT

Fruit juice is loaded with sugar, but if you blend the whole fruit, then you are also drinking the enzymes and fiber in addition to the vitamins and minerals.

THE NEW PANTRY: FROM SCOBIES TO TASTE-TRIPPERS

While your mocktails and cocktails will be bursting with fresh plant life and—if you're alcoholically inclined—a selection of mid-range quality spirits, there are a few useful staples to keep in your cupboard. As the book includes forays into fermentation and cultured drinks, I've also included ingredients to get you started down that route. There are also a few surprises such as miracle berries and chickpea water.

ALCOHOL OVER 80 PROOF/40% ABV

I would suggest storing some strong, neutral-tasting alcohol such as vodka that you can use for a variety of purposes—for infusing fresh and dried plants, making tinctures and bitters, and increasing the shelf life of cordials and syrups.

BITTERS

This is a seasoning for drinks and an important part of many cocktails. Bitters contain tiny amounts of alcohol, so, if you are allowing yourself a few drops, you'll find they really liven up a mocktail. There are many small-batch artisanal bitters to choose from or you can make your own. For example, try making Citrus Bitters (see page 75) or Becky's Windfall Bitters (see page 77).

CHICKPEA WATER

If you are vegan, or just want to try something new, chickpea water (or aquafaba) is a fantastic foam maker. This discovery was made in 2014 by French chef Joel Roessel who found that if you boil the water from canned chickpeas (garbanzo beans) or other beans, the proteins, carbohydrates, and plant solids have an emulsifying and thickening action. Try using chickpea water in the Sherry and Aquafaba Aperitif (see page 158). It really does work beautifully and doesn't taste of chickpeas.

CITRIC ACID

You can easily source citric acid in powdered form online or at a health food or homebrewing store. Citric acid is great for increasing the shelf life of low alcohol or non-alcoholic infusions and syrups. It also provides a low level of acidity, which means you often don't need to add any fresh citrus to a drink. Simply follow the instructions on the label.

COCONUT MILK

While coconut milk (the thicker strained juice from coconut flesh) is quite fatty, it's also bursting with nutrients and is great for lactose-intolerant people wishing to make kefir (see Coconut Milk Kefir, on page 128). It has a creamy texture and natural sweetness. Because coconut milk is completely free of dairy, lactose, soy, nuts, or grains, it's also a good option for anyone who's allergic to dairy and nut- or grain-based milks, plus it's vegan and good for plant-based eaters. While coconut water is higher in sugar and certain electrolytes, coconut milk contains a beneficial fat called lauric acid, which is easily absorbed and used by the body for energy. Just use it sparingly! Try it in the Virgin and Vegan Piña Colada (see page 140).

apple mint

HERBS

It is useful to have a selection of herbs at hand for making a range of drinks, especially cold- and hot-brewed teas. To prolong their shelf life, herbs can either be frozen or dried. Fresh herbs can be frozen in ice-cube trays filled with water. Once frozen, transfer the herb cubes to airtight containers and store in the freezer until needed. They

DRYING HERBS

Drying amplifies the flavor of certain herbs, such as those containing coumarin (e.g. meadowsweet and sweet woodruff) which gives a wonderful scent of newly mown hay. It is important to dry herbs containing coumarin quickly to prevent a toxic mold forming. In any case, most herbs benefit from a swift drying process. Here are a few tips on drying herbs:

To dry soft herbs swiftly, place the freshly picked fresh herbs in a single layer on a baking sheet. Place in an oven heated to the lowest possible setting until the herbs are brittle or crumble easily (check them regularly). You can even leave the oven door open if you don't mind overheating yourself! Store the dried herbs in a cool, dry place away from sunlight, moisture, and heat. Most dried herbs diminish in flavor after a year.

For a slower drying of soft herbs, spread them on paper towels or a clean dishtowel in a single layer until any moisture has evaporated. Tie the herbs in small bundles by their stems and hang them upside down in a warm, dry place, ensuring plenty of air can circulate around each bunch.

To collect herb seeds (e.g. fennel seeds), pick a stem with seedheads. Place a brown paper bag with a few holes snipped in the sides over the seedhead. Place the bag somewhere dark, but with good air circulation, and collect the seeds when they are fully dry. Store the dried seeds in a labeled airtight container away from sunlight.

EDIBLE-GRADE ESSENTIAL OILS

It takes serious equipment and thousands of blossoms to make just 5mg of high-grade essential oil, so buying this type of oil is expensive. But pure oils are a viable alternative if you wish to capture all the volatile oils, scent, flavor, and medical constituents of your favorite plants.

EGGS

Mouth-feel is an important part of a mocktail or cocktail, so it's fun to put a foam on top of a drink occasionally. Egg whites provide a tasteless, frothy, creamy foam with a pleasant mouth-feel that creates a wonderful, white platform for bitters or a garnish, to prevent it sinking to the bottom of the glass. Eggs also add a mild element if you need to balance strong, sweet, and sour elements. Always use fresh organic eggs. Chickpea water (see page 17) makes a good vegan alternative.

FILTERED OR DISTILLED WATER

If you're going down the "cultured route" of fermented drinks, you will need filtered or distilled water because the chlorine, fluoride, and other chemicals in tap water will destroy the healthy yeasts and bacteria you are trying to grow. Even mineral or spring water contain minerals that may harm your cultures over time. Some pharmacists supply distilled water or you can fit a filtering water-kit at home.

will be great for infusions, but not garnishes. For leaves, berries, and some petals, you can store the plant material on baking sheets, or in glass jars or Ziploc bags, in the freezer until needed. For guidance on drying herbs, see the Drying Herbs box, opposite.

KEFIR GRAINS

There are two types of kefir grains: milk kefir grains and water kefir grains. These are not really grains (they just resemble them), but a colony of yeast and bacteria that can be used to make probiotic drinks, namely Water Kefir (see page 126) and Cow's Milk Kefir (see page 128). You will need to keep the grains in the refrigerator between uses.

MIRACLE BERRIES

Native to west and central Africa, miracle berries from the tropical evergreen shrub *Synsepalum dulcificum* offer an incredible taste sensation that can be fun at parties—though if food miles bother you, they might not be for you. These berries are now being grown in experimental plantations in tropical America and have been introduced to many Southeast Asian countries and Australia. They are tasteless themselves, but have a sweetening effect on sour foods, to the extent that you can suck on the sourest lemon and it will taste of sherbet. This sensation occurs because an active glycoprotein molecule called miraculin attaches to your taste buds, alters the sweet receptors on your tongue, and changes sour flavors to sweet flavors. The effect can last 5–30 minutes. The point being that you can avoid using sugar in mixed drinks, but "increase" their sweetness by eating some miracle berries first.

OILS

Back to mouth-feel, a few drops of oil on the surface of a drink, or emulsified in the drink, can create a really interesting texture. The oils themselves also carry flavors beautifully. You can also drop bitters onto the oils for a concentrated burst of flavor and for an interesting garnish. Try combing the floating oil into a pattern (my mother was a paper marbler and this was a major part of the process—she'd be proud I've found a medium to carry on the family tradition!). Try using Sage-infused Hazelnut Oil (see page 86) in Into The Woods (see page 170).

ROOTS AND BARK

It is illegal in the U.K. and many other countries to pick anything by the root when foraging. For this reason, only people who are absolutely sure of what they are picking, and have permission to do so, should forage roots or bark. As an alternative, I suggest ordering roots and bark from reputable online suppliers. They make fantastic bittering agents, with wonderful medicinal properties, and can be kept in airtight containers in the pantry until needed.

SCOBIES

If you get as addicted to making kombucha as me, you'll want to play with a SCOBY (Symbiotic Culture of Bacteria and Yeast). It will do wonders for your gut health and make some delicious drinks. You can buy SCOBIES online, but I would recommend finding someone nearby willing to donate a "baby" SCOBY from the "mother," so it doesn't go through the trauma and starvation of traveling by post! For more advice on sourcing and caring for your SCOBY, see Simple Kombucha, on page 122).

SPARKLING WATER

Sparkling water should be your go-to mixer if you want to keep calories to a minimum and avoid high sugar-level tonics and sodas. It gives a pleasing fizz and sparkle to mocktails and cocktails. Buy smaller bottles, so they aren't wasted when they go flat.

SUGAR ALTERNATIVES

There are many unrefined sugar alternatives to grow, forage, or buy, so look back to the section on Healthy Alternatives to Sugar (see pages 14–15) for suggestions.

TEAS

There is an exciting abundance of tea flavors, whether they are true teas or tisanes, using a mélange of plants. Disposable teabags are a great way to infuse flavor into liquor or to make cold-brew teas without the fuss of straining. If you use Lapsang Souchong tea, you can even impart smokiness to your cocktails without needing a smoker. Sample this in the Lemongrass, Pineapple Weed, and Szechuan Teagroni (see page 108).

VINEGARS

Vinegars are great in shrubs like the Strawberry, Clover, and Meadowsweet Shrub (see page 84) or simply to carry flavor, as in the Magnolia Flower Vinegar (see page 81). Apple cider vinegar has the most health benefits, but opt for champagne or white wine vinegar for quality of flavor.

COCKTAIL-MAKING EQUIPMENT

You will probably already have a lot of the tools and equipment listed here in your kitchen cupboards, especially if you enjoy cooking or making homemade drinks. However, if you are missing anything, these pieces are all available from good kitchen stores and online suppliers.

BASIC EQUIPMENT

You can usually improvise or supplement most equipment, but certain tools will make life easier and you're likely to already have, or be able to source, most of them easily and cheaply.

Blender This is great for making margaritas and non-alcoholic, blended ice drinks. A top tip is to blend your ice first—to fully break it up—and then the fruit/liquor/juices/milks to ensure everything is blended smoothly.

Bottles and jars Hoard jars of every shape and size. Ideally, you need a range of sizes, including wide-mouthed, sealable, 1-quart (1-liter) glass jars such as Kilner or Mason jars. Little jelly (jam) jars and smaller jars are useful for tinctures and freezing herbs.

Coffee filters/AeroPress® coffee filter I use an AeroPress® coffee filter to ensure the clearest infusions with the fewest particles, but paper coffee filters do the same job as muslin or cheesecloth (when used with a fine-mesh strainer) for avoiding sediment in your infusions. I sometimes use a gold coffee filter when straining because it is reusable.

Coffee grinder Great for grinding spices, dried mushrooms, and all sorts.

Fine-mesh strainer Like a chinois, for straining very small particles from infusions.

Funnel You need one that is thinner than the top of your presentation bottle to get your infusion from the wide-mouthed pitcher into the finished bottle.

Glass presentation bottles Try to find a selection, ranging in volume from ½ pint (250ml) to 1 quart (1 liter).

Heavy-bottomed, nonreactive saucepans It is important when you are using acidic ingredients, such as citrus juice and fruit, and strongly colored vegetables, to avoid pans made with aluminum, tin, or unlined copper—the pan lining will become stained and possibly pit and peel off.

Labels or pen You will get irritated very quickly if you cannot find a label or a pen that works on glass. Remember to include the date and the contents on your bottled treasures.

Muslin/cheesecloth You really want to avoid sediment in the bottom of your creations because over time that organic matter festers. It also looks good to get it out. Several layers of clean muslin or cheesecloth inside a fine-mesh strainer can get your liquid as particle-free as it needs to be.

Wide-mouthed pitcher/jug Used for funneling infusions from a pan.

SPECIALIST COCKTAIL EQUIPMENT

The items listed here are not essential—you can always improvise. However, they are fun, useful, and make cocktail-making tasks more enjoyable.

Barspoon This multipurpose tool is cheap and fulfills a lot of different functions. It is designed to measure 1 barspoon (5ml). It stirs, mixes, muddles, and scoops, and is great for long glasses.

Blowtorch Catering blowtorches are great for jobs like grilling fruit (see the Toasted Kumquat and Amaretto Sour, on page 164) or for scorching herbs to give a smoky taste to a cocktail.

Cocktail shaker There are several types. I prefer a Boston shaker, which is simply a pint-sized mixing glass with a slightly larger metal tin that fits on top. You will need a separate strainer. Alternatively, you can use a Cobbler shaker, which has an integrated strainer that is part of the lid, a tall glass, and a cap. Whichever shaker you buy, you simply fill the cocktail shaker two-thirds of the way up with ice, add your ingredients, cover, and shake. When the Boston shaker tin becomes frosty with condensation, your drink is cold enough to strain.

Cold-brew teapot Again, this is not essential but is designed to make your cold-brew tea very easy to make; there is a built-in filter so you don't have to strain your teas.

Cutting board and sharp knife Essential kit for prepping cocktail ingredients and garnishes.

Dehydrater These are useful for making garnishes—for example, the dried quince in the Quince Delight (see page 160). Borrow one from a friend, if need be.

Digital scales, pipettes, small dropper/apothecary bottles, and labels If you are interested in making bitters and tinctures, you will find a set of digital scales very useful for measuring the minute quantities that are needed. They are surprisingly cheap to buy. You will also need a pipette, small dropper or apothecary bottles, and labels for your final creations.

Hawthorne strainer This is the ideal strainer for a Boston shaker, as it is designed to fit over it perfectly. It is made of stainless steel with spring-loaded coil around the perimeter to hold back ice and large particles of fruit or herbs as you pour into the cocktail glass. A top tip for making a foam using egg white is to put the spring-loaded coil into the cocktail shaker, seal, and shake. It really helps emulsify the mix and speeds up the time it takes to create a lovely foam.

Ice bucket and ice scoop/tongs If you're with close friends or family, you can probably omit these, but everyone else will expect you to use a scoop or some tongs for your cocktails. An ice bucket is useful for group gatherings.

Jigger This is used for pouring cocktails accurately. It is made of two "thimbles" that are joined together, with one thimble measuring 1oz (30ml), or a "pony shot," and the other measuring 1½oz (45ml), or a "standard" or "jigger" shot.

Julep strainer As the name suggests, this is the classic strainer for Juleps and is kept in the drink while you sip, to hold back the crushed ice. It basically looks like a domed metal spoon with holes in it. A julep strainer is also used to strain other drinks that are stirred in a mixing glass, as opposed to shaken.

Mixing glass A Boston shaker will already come with this glass, but there are plenty of attractive and/or vintage ones if you want to get fancy. A mixing glass of some sort is essential for drinks that need to be stirred, not shaken.

Muddler You can improvise with the disc end of a barspoon or the end of a wooden spoon, but a muddler is tall and skinny enough to fit in a long glass, yet wide enough to add

Kilner jar

some oomph when muddling fruit or herbs. Personally, I prefer to "smack" herbs to release their essential oils rather than bruise them with muddling (see page 24).

Professional cream whipper (with N2O cartridges) With this baby you can make instant infusions using nitrous oxide cartridges. Always follow the manufacturer's instructions carefully.

Soda maker (with CO2 cartridges) Not only can you make your own sodas with this piece of equipment—try it for the Wild Sour Cherry and Flowering Currant Soda (see page 80), but you can also use it to make your own sparkling water and so save money! The CO2 cartridges will make your drinks properly fizzy.

Tea strainer Sometimes you need to double-strain your cocktail to catch tiny particles of ice, herbs, and fruit that won't be caught by the shaker's strainer or the hawthorne/julep strainer. A regular tea strainer does the job nicely.

Tweezers/tongs Useful for handling edible flowers or herbs in long, thin glasses. The best type to get hold of are the long ones used by sushi/sous chefs, so you can reach the bottom of the glass.

GLASSWARE

Glassware doesn't just look good; it serves a purpose. For example, as plants feature heavily in garnishes in the long drinks, it's a good idea to use tall, thin Highball/Collins glasses that are not much wider than your ice cubes. This means you can stack the ice cubes on top of each other and push the flower and herb garnishes to the sides where they will be clearly visible—instead of them getting lost in the middle of the glass or sinking to the bottom.

Shorter drinks that contain a lot of alcohol and no mixer, such as a Martini, are best served in smaller Martini, coupe, or sherry glasses. Otherwise, you will be tempted to serve much larger portions of alcohol than is safe or will only fill a larger glass half-full. It's much better to serve a smaller amount of high-quality spirits and beautiful ingredients than a larger amount of lower quality.

1 Wine glass
2 Champagne flute
3 Balloon cup
4 Highball
5 Collins
6 Rocks
7 Martini
8 Sherry

Balloon cup: Increasingly, these large balloon cup or Copa de Balon glasses are the preferred choice for gin and tonic or even for spritz aperitifs, but they were traditionally used for red wine, allowing for maximum access to oxygen, and therefore maximum aroma and flavor. The glass is designed to trap the aromas of the gin to give a better taste to the drink, but the large bowl also allows plenty of ice and lime into the glass to add to the flavor and keep the drink cool. Crucially, though, the bowl shape is said to stop the ice cubes from melting too quickly.

Champagne flute: Long, narrow-stemmed glass that is used to serve sparkling wine.

Collins/Highball: These are perfect for serving long drinks over ice with a mixer. I try to use a 10-oz (300-ml) or 12-oz (360-ml) Collins glass for most long drinks.

Coupe/Saucer: These are beautiful, bowl-shaped glasses, traditionally used for Champagne, but also great for Martinis, sours, and other cocktails. I prefer using a small 5-oz (150-ml) coupe glass.

Martini: Also known as a cocktail glass, this is the classic cone-shaped glass with a stem. I use a 5-oz (150-ml) glass for most Martinis and sours.

Old Fashioned/Rocks: These are great for serving Negronis or short drinks over ice—that is, "on the rocks." They are a short, wide, heavy-bottomed glass in which you can use larger ice cubes to slow down the melting time.

Sherry: Sherry glasses are smaller glasses that are great for reducing cocktail sizes generally. You can pick up gorgeous, mismatched vintage sherry glasses at thrift stores.

ICE

Ice serves two purposes: it cools the drink down, but also dilutes it—and the latter is important. In a really strong cocktail, shaken or stirred, you want about 25 percent of the liquid you pour into the final serve to be iced water. It balances out the strong ingredients. However, sometimes, while you may want the drink served as cold as possible, you also want to delay the ice melting. For example, a Negroni containing a mix of gin, Campari, and vermouth is best served in a rocks glass with the largest ice cube you can find, to slow down the dilution time.

In this book, I have used regular ice cubes for shaking, stirring, and serving. You can also buy silicon molds for making much larger cubes and spheres, which create beautiful shapes, and you can certainly play around with them in different ways—for example, using them to freeze mixers such as birch sap, juice, or coconut milk, or filling the ice tray with blossoms, berries, or leaves.

For really clear ice cubes, boil distilled water and let cool before repeating the process. Pour the cooled water into the ice-cube tray and freeze in a closed container so the ice doesn't pick up other flavors in the freezer.

To freeze flowers within an ice cube, use double-boiled distilled water, if possible, to ensure you get crystal-clear ice cubes. Half-fill each mold of the ice-cube tray with water, put the blossom, leaves, or berries in the cubes, and place the tray in the freezer. Let freeze before filling the rest of the cubes with the remaining cooled boiled water and returning to the freezer until required.

TECHNIQUES

Whether you are a complete novice at mixing drinks or have a little experience, following the techniques outlined here will help you to become more proficient and create the best-tasting mocktails and cocktails. With practice, these techniques will soon become second nature.

MEASURING

If you wish, you can work in "parts" rather than ounces or milliliters to work out ratios. Whichever method you choose, it's a good idea for balance and consistency to measure accurately, especially when you devise a recipe you want to repeat. The smallest changes can knock a recipe out.

MUDDLING

If you don't have a muddler, you can use the disc end of a barspoon or the end of a wooden spoon instead. Muddling lightly crushes ingredients like citrus or other fruits to release their juices. Muddling can bruise some ingredients, however, releasing unwanted bitterness into a drink, so I prefer to "smack" herbs in the palm of my hand to release their essential oils before dropping them into the cocktail shaker or mixing glass.

SHAKING

If your drink contains citrus, or liquids that have a wide variety of viscosity (e.g. a thin spirit and a thick syrup, or dairy or chickpea water), you need to shake your cocktail. Shaking thoroughly combines the ingredients, so you don't get layered flavors and textures in a drink. It also makes your drink colder and more diluted. Fill a shaker two-thirds of the way up with ice. Add the ingredients, seal the shaker, and shake hard for 20 seconds. If you are using egg white or chickpea water, either shake harder for another 10 seconds or, alternatively, take the coiled spring from a hawthorne strainer and drop it into the cocktail mix before sealing and shaking—this will help emulsify the mix in a regular 20-second shake. Remember to put the spring back on the hawthorne strainer before straining and serving!

STERILIZING

Wash bottles and jars, and other pieces of equipment that need sterilizing, in very hot, soapy water, then dry them in an oven set to a low temperature. Alternatively, you can use some sterilizing solution/tablets, following the manufacturer's instructions on the label. This method is ideal for sterilizing equipment such as metal or wooden

stirring in a mixing glass

utensils. Either way, you are probably using organic ingredients, so it's important that your storage jars and bottles are sterilized before use.

STIRRING

If your cocktail is pure spirits and liquids of roughly the same viscosity (e.g. vermouth and wine), there is no need to shake, as shaking will make your drink slightly cloudy. Instead, pour the ingredients into a regular mixing glass or the metal half of a Boston shaker. Fill the mixing glass two-thirds of the way up with ice. Use a long-handled barspoon or the handle of a wooden spoon to stir the ingredients for about 20 seconds or until condensation appears on the outside of the glass. Strain and serve.

STRAINING

To serve a clear, particle-free cocktail, place a strainer over the mouth of the shaker or mixing glass to hold back the ice and any pieces of fruit and herbs, while you pour the liquid into the glass.

Fine-straining When you're bottling infusions it is important to keep them as particle- and sediment-free as possible, to preserve their flavor, shelf life, and looks. Rather than just using a kitchen sieve, a fine-mesh strainer, such as a chinois, can be placed over a wide-mouthed pitcher or jar and a few layers of muslin/cheesecloth placed inside to catch the smallest particles. Alternatively, you can line the fine-mesh strainer with coffee filters, passing the infusion through them to achieve equally great results.

Double-straining To double-strain, place a strainer over the mouth of the shaker or mixing glass held in one hand, while holding a tea strainer in the other hand directly over the cocktail glass. Pour the mix through the main strainer and also through the tea strainer to double-strain/catch any remaining ice particles or pieces of herb and fruit.

WASHING INGREDIENTS

All fruit/vegetable/plant/herb ingredients should be washed before use, particularly foraged plants.

muslin, chinois, and Kilner jar

Caution: The plants and herbs listed in this section are powerful. They should be eaten in moderation and monitored for any allergic reactions that occur on ingestion. If you are taking other medication, are suffering from a medical condition, or are pregnant, breastfeeding, or have/had breast cancer, do not take any of the herbs (as many can affect hormone balance and cause uterine contractions, or are estrogenic).

CHAPTER 2

PLANTS WITH BENEFITS:
HEALTH, FLAVOR, AND GOOD LOOKS

We are becoming increasingly aware of the nutritional and taste limits of our modern diet. It's true that you can source most fruit, vegetables, and herbs all year round in metropolitan cities, but at what cost taste-wise, nutritionally, and environmentally? Often the produce will have been forced under glass and bred for shape, disease-tolerance, or an ability to withstand storage and travel across continents, rather than for flavor or nutritional value. The other option—and one that brings numerous health benefits and flavors, as well as the pleasure of tending beautiful plants—is to grow natural ingredients in your own garden and use them in homemade drinks. Even more exciting for me—and possibly for you—is foraging in the wild for your own free ingredients.

   This chapter contains helpful information on a few garden and foraged plants. Some are interchangeable—that is, they are garden or "introduced" plants that have naturalized in the wild, where you can forage for them, or are wild plants that have happily found their way into gardens. Where possible, I've highlighted recipes in the book in which they can be used. If these plants are unavailable to you, I have also suggested a commercial alternative where one exists.

PLANTS FROM THE GARDEN

Part of the joy of making your own mocktails and cocktails is growing unusual ingredients that are delicious, packed with nutrients, inexpensive to grow, hard to find commercially, stunning to look at, beautiful to smell, and gorgeous to taste. Here are just a few of my favorite garden plants for using in a wide range of wonderful libations.

Aloysia citrodora
LEMON VERBENA

A native of South America, lemon verbena is a deciduous sub-shrub with aromatic leaves and tiny white or pale lilac flowers.

Where to grow: Full sun and well-drained soil. Can be grown in temperate climates, as long as it is given winter protection.

Taste profile: Incredible lemony scent and taste that intensifies when the leaves are touched or bruised.

Health benefits: Powerful antioxidant properties and antidepressant compounds. Used to aid weight loss, protect muscles, reduce inflammation, boost the immune system, calm the stomach, reduce fevers, soothe nerves, and clear up congestion.

Store-bought alternatives: Mint or lemons

Suggested recipes: Blackcurrant Sage, Winter Savory, and Lemon Verbena Tea (see page 97), Strawberry and Lemon Verbena Mocktail (see page 142)

Angelica archangelica
ANGELICA

A tall, architectural perennial with huge umbels of light yellow flowers in early summer, turning to aromatic seedpods. Found naturally in riverbeds and moist hedgerows in Europe, Asia, and North America.

Where to grow: Prefers moist, fertile soil in full or partial shade.

Taste profile: Parsley-flavored green leaves and licorice-flavored seeds, which can be added to rhubarb as a natural sweetener or to bitters, vermouth, and other alcohol infusions for their aromatic and herbal notes.

Health benefits: Aphrodisiac, antibacterial, and antifungal properties and a general digestive and tonic.

Store-bought alternatives: Parsley and dill-weed, juniper berries

Suggested recipes: Wild Homemade Aquavit (see page 64), Citrus Bitters (see page 75), Citrus Amaro (see page 87)

Artemisia absinthium
WORMWOOD

Native to Europe and Asia, this woody perennial has silvery gray, aromatic foliage. The leaves are finely divided.

Where to grow: Prefers full sun and well-drained soil.

Taste profile: Intense bitterness

Health benefits: The bitter components and acids in the leaves, flowers, and roots are excellent for relieving indigestion. Also used to treat fever, and as a tonic and aphrodisiac.

Store-bought alternative: None

Suggested recipe: Wild Dry Vermouth (see page 55)

Borago officinalis
BORAGE

A hardy annual native to Europe, with delightful blue and, occasionally, purple and white, star-shaped flowers.

Where to grow: Happy in any sunny spot in poor, well-drained soil.

Taste profile: Borage leaves (and teas made from them) have a cucumber flavor.

Health benefits: Borage leaf tea is said to be good for reducing high

lemon verbena

temperatures. The leaves and flowers are rich in potassium and calcium, making them good for purifying the blood and as a general tonic.

Store-bought alternative: Cucumber

Suggested recipe: As a garnish for Lemongrass Leaftini Mocktail (see page 106)

Cydonia oblonga
QUINCE

Belonging to the same family as apples and pears, quince are shaped like pears, but are larger. Native to Southwest Asia, they have lumpy, yellow skin and a hard flesh that is inedible unless cooked, although you can infuse raw quince dipped in lemon in alcohol.

Where to grow: Grows best in deep, fertile, moisture-retentive soil. Although hardy, a warm, sunny, sheltered spot is required, as quince flowers are susceptible to frost and sun is needed for the fruit to ripen.

Taste profile: When cooked, tastes like a floral, perfume-y apple or pear crossed with melon.

Health benefits: Quince are a rich source of vitamin C, zinc, potassium, copper, iron, and dietary fiber. Also rich in organic compounds, including catechin, epicatechin, and limonene, plus other phytonutrients. Together these stimulate hair follicles, boost the immune system, improve skin condition and digestive health, and help maintain normal blood pressure.

Store-bought alternative: Pears

Suggested recipes: Quince Vodka with Szechuan Pepper, Star Anise, and Juniper Berries (see page 52), Roast Quince, Szechuan Pepper, Juniper, and Star Anise Mocktail (see page 138), Quince Delight (see page 160)

Cymbopogon citratus
LEMONGRASS

This tropical perennial grass, native to Southeast Asia, has flat, gray-green leaves that can grow up to 3ft (1m) long.

Where to grow: Grows in temperate conditions, but is only half-hardy, so needs winter protection. Requires hot, wet summers and warm, dry winters to thrive.

Taste profile: Fresh lemongrass has a vibrant lemon scent and taste, but with a mild sweetness and none of the sourness or tartness of lemon juice.

Health benefits: Like lemon balm (*Melissa officinalis*), lemongrass has been used for over 2,000 years. Lemongrass tea has stimulant properties. Some people use the citronellol in lemongrass to lower blood pressure or reduce fever. Lemongrass tea reduces the "munchies" if you want to curb calories.

Store-bought alternative: Dried lemongrass

Suggested recipes: Lemongrass Tea (see page 99), Lemongrass Leaftini Mocktail (see page 106), Lemongrass, Pineapple Weed, and Szechuan Teagroni (see page 108), Lemongrass, Jasmine Green Tea, and Sake Punch (see page 112), Roast Rhubarb, Blood Orange, Sweet Cicely, and Lemongrass Mocktail (see page 139)

Ficus carica
FIG

A deciduous bush or small tree, originating from Western Asia and the eastern Mediterranean, it has broad leaves and succulent fruits. There are hundreds of varieties.

borage

Some crop just once in early to mid-summer, while others bear a second crop in late summer/fall (autumn).

Where to grow: Tolerates a variety of soil types, but needs good drainage and full sun.

Taste profile: Fruity, sweet, and aromatic, but not juicy, with a pulpy, seedy, jelly-like flesh.

Health benefits: High in fiber and contains significant amounts of calcium, potassium, phosphorus, and iron.

Store-bought alternatives: Plenty available

Suggested recipes: Cherry and Cacao Liquore (see page 90), Water Kefir (see page 126)

Fragaria
STRAWBERRY

This fleshy, juicy, summer fruit grows from runners/stolons, which put down new roots to produce cloned plants.

Where to grow: Prefers full sun, but can tolerate a bit of shade. The alpine strawberry (*Fragaria vesca*) prefers partial shade.

lavender

Taste profile: Sweet, jammy, juicy, fresh, rosy, floral.

Health benefits: Packed with vitamin C, antioxidants, and fiber. Eight strawberries contain 120 percent of the recommended daily intake of vitamin C. Research suggests they can contribute to the lowering of blood-cholesterol levels and decrease the spike in blood-sugar levels after high-sugar meals.

Store-bought alternatives: Plenty available

Suggested recipes: Strawberry, Clover, and Meadowsweet Shrub (see page 84), Coconut Water Kefir Strawberry Cosmo (see page 141), Strawberry and Lemon Verbena Mocktail (see page 142), Hot Strawberry Fizz (see page 163)

Glycyrrhiza glabra
LICORICE

Native to southern Europe and parts of Asia, the roots of this herbaceous perennial legume are widely prized.

Where to grow: Prefers sandy soil near water and a hot, dry situation.

Taste profile: Musky, lingering, sweet flavor—but not a very strong taste of licorice! The root in dried form is used as a sweetener.

Health benefits: Contains many antidepressant compounds. The key therapeutic compound in the root—glycyrrhizin (which is 50 times sweeter than sugar)—prevents the breakdown of adrenal hormones such as cortisol, so helping combat stress. It is also used to treat ulcers. It can lower stomach-acid levels and relieve heartburn, indigestion, and constipation. Eases congestion. May also block artery-clogging, plaque buildup, so contributing to healthy heart function.

Store-bought alternative: Commercial licorice syrups

Suggested recipes: Wild Homemade Aquavit (see page 64), Thyme and Licorice Syrup (see page 73)

Hypericum androsaemum
TUTSAN

A semi-evergreen shrub with yellow flowers, found growing in Europe, North Africa, and western Asia. The berries, which turn from white/green to red to black, are poisonous. It's the leaves that are used.

Where to grow: Damp hedgerows and woodland are the plant's natural habitat, so prefers moist, humus-rich soil.

Taste profile: The leaves have a gorgeous scent when dried and hold that scent for years. In his book *Flora Britannica*, Richard Mabey says the leaves have "an evocative, fugitive scent, reminiscent of cigar boxes and candied fruit." Some liken the scent to ambergris, so it is often known as sweet amber.

Health benefits: Closely related to St John's wort, it can be used to clean wounds and aid healing as an antiseptic.

Store-bought alternatives: None

Suggested recipe: Oaked Vodka (see page 48)

Lavandula
LAVENDER

This small evergreen shrub, with aromatic leaves, is largely native to northern Africa and the mountainous regions of the Mediterranean.

Where to grow: Grows happily in full sun in poor soils with excellent drainage.

Taste profile: Floral, pungent aroma; woody, earthy, with an undertone of mint.

Health benefits: The essential oils from the flowers are extracted for use in teas and other infusions. Excellent for depression, restlessness, anxiety, and insomnia. Also has antifungal and antibacterial properties. Soothing for upset stomach, digestive disorders, intestinal gas, and nausea.

Store-bought alternative: Commercial lavender

Suggested recipe: Ginger, Lemon, and Lavender Kombucha (see page 124)

Magnolia officinalis
MAGNOLIA

Native to China, this spectacular tree can withstand temperatures down to 14°F (-10°C). Goblet-shaped, white/pale pink, fragrant flowers appear in spring.

Where to grow: Full sun and moist, fertile soil.

Taste profile: Petals smell fragrant and spicy, have a glaucous texture, and taste a little like rose petals. If you pickle them, they taste of ginger. The bark is highly aromatic.

Health benefits: The bark has been used for thousands of years, particularly in Chinese medicine, to treat a variety of ailments, including asthma, but the flower buds can also be used with the bark to treat coughs, colds, and intestinal problems. Magnolia bark has been getting a lot of attention recently as an ingredient in a supplement that reduces levels of the stress hormone cortisol. It also has a positive effect on acetylcholine levels in the brain, offering potential benefits to people suffering from Alzheimer's disease.

Store-bought alternatives: Ginger or rose petals

Suggested recipes: Magnolia Flower Vinegar (see page 81), Magnolia and Cherry Blossom Shrub (see page 83)

Melissa officinalis
LEMON BALM

Perennial herbaceous herb native to the southern Mediterranean, the Middle East, and parts of central Asia, but now naturalized in the U.S., U.K., and many other places.

Where to grow: Full sun or partial shade and well-drained soil.

Taste profile: Lemon

Health benefits: This wonder herb has been used for over 2,000 years for both its sedative and cerebral-stimulating effects. It also has antibacterial and antioxidant properties, so has been used to treat everything, including flu, fever, mood disorders, palpitations, toothache, and vomiting. Also great for sleeping problems and menstrual cramps.

The essential oils are proven to have a sedative action on the nervous system. Greatly increases the ability to concentrate and perform word and picture tests. Its antioxidants protect the body's cells, including those in the brain, from oxidation.

Store-bought alternative: Mint

Suggested recipes: As an ingredient in cold-brew tea (see page 94) and as a garnish in Lemongrass, Jasmine Green Tea, and Sake Punch (see page 112)

Mentha piperata f. citrata
CHOCOLATE MINT

A perennial herb grown for its leaves, which smell and taste rather like "After Eight" mints.

Where to grow: Rich, moist soil in full sun or partial shade.

Taste profile: See above!

Health benefits: Great appetizer and palate cleanser. Also promotes digestion and soothes indigestion, inflammation, and nausea. Cooling and calming.

Store-bought alternatives: Spearmint or peppermint

Suggested recipe: Citrus Amaro (see page 87)

Monarda didyma
BERGAMOT, BEE BALM

This perennial member of the mint family is native to North America. *Monarda didyma* has tubular, scarlet flowers clustered in pom-pom-shaped whorls in summer.

Where to grow: Full sun and moist, well-drained soil.

bergamot

Taste profile: *Monarda didyma* petals taste citrusy, peppery, and like Earl Grey tea. The crushed leaves are slightly more bitter and hotter—like oregano crossed with spearmint—so it is best to use the petals in teas.

Health benefits: First Nation Americans used the crushed leaves of *Monarda didyma* and *M. fistulosa* to make Oswego tea, to soothe digestive orders. *Monarda* contains thymol, a natural ingredient used in mouthwash, which has powerful antibacterial properties. The leaves and flowers are useful for easing colds and reducing fever, as well as soothing sore throats, headaches, insomnia, and menstrual pain.

Store-bought alternatives: Oregano, bergamot orange, spearmint

Suggested recipe: As an ingredient in a hot-brew tea (see page 95)

Myrrhis odorata
SWEET CICELY

An aromatic herbaceous perennial, native to Europe, with gorgeous, fern-like leaves in spring and umbels of small, white flowers in early summer. These are followed by long, thin, aniseed-scented, brown-ribbed seeds in late summer. You might get new growth again in the fall (autumn). Not to be confused with the *Osmorhiza* genus, which is native to Asia and the American continents, and also called "sweet cicely."

Where to grow: Prefers moderately fertile, moist, but well-drained soil in dappled shade.

Taste profile: The leaves, seeds, and roots have a strong, sweet, anise flavor. Great with rhubarb.

Health benefits: The leaves stimulate appetite. Steeping the leaves in tea for 15 minutes is great for easing menstrual cramps. If you add a bit of ginger to the tea, you will also aid digestion, cure flatulence, and be generally uplifted! You can make a decoction with the roots, which acts as both a stimulant and a relaxant due to its antispasmodic properties.

The flavonoids in the plant act as an antiseptic and help purify the blood.

Store-bought alternatives: Fennel, licorice

Suggested recipes: Wild Homemade Aquavit (see page 64), Roast Rhubarb, Blood Orange, Sweet Cicely, and Lemongrass Mocktail (see page 139), and as a garnish in Strawberry and Lemon Verbena Mocktail (see page 142)

Oxalis acetosella
WOOD SORREL

Common in North America, Europe, and Asia, this rhizomatous perennial is found in woodland and shady places. It has clover-like leaves and delicate, white/pink flowers from spring to mid-summer.

Where to grow: Prefers partial shade and humus-rich soil.

Taste profile: Lemony, sour

Health benefits: High in vitamin C. A thirst-quencher and appetite stimulant. The leaves, flowers, green pods, and roots are all edible, soothing the stomach, relieving indigestion, and helping prevent vomiting.

Store-bought alternative: None

Suggested recipe: Iced Spring Tonic Tea (see page 100)

Pelargonium
SCENTED GERANIUM

A semi-woody tender perennial, largely from South Africa, the leaves of different varieties display a range of shapes, sizes, and colors. The small flowers vary from white, through pink, to red.

Where to grow: Full sun and a well-drained, composted site. Rarely survives a cold winter.

Taste profile: Aromatic foliage with a range of scents, from lemon to orange to rose to cola!

Health benefits: The aroma is uplifting. Drinking tea made from scented geraniums can have a calming effect, similar to that of chamomile, and may help reduce stress and anxiety. The tea can be used to clean the face and is thought to combat pimples and acne due to its antibacterial properties. When ingested, scented geranium can relieve stomach ache, diarrhea, and headaches.

Store-bought alternatives: Lemons, mint

Suggested recipe: Pineapple Sage and Scented Geranium Tea (see page 96)

Ribes nigrum
BLACKCURRANT

This woody shrub is native to the temperate parts of central and northern Europe and also northern Asia.

Where to grow: Prefers full sun and damp fertile soils.

Taste profile: As well as the familiar fruits, the leaves are strongly aromatic and taste of blackcurrant when used fresh.

Health benefits: Powerful antioxidant with anti-inflammatory properties and also a good flu-buster.

Store-bought alternative: Blackcurrants

Suggested recipe: Wild Cherry, Rose, and Cacao Nib Vodka (see Variation, page 47)

sweet cicely

Ribes sanguineum
FLOWERING CURRANT

An upright deciduous shrub, with beautiful, pink racemes in spring. It is native to western U.S. and Canada, but grows prolifically in gardens and has been naturalized in parts of the U.K.

Where to grow: Full sun and moderately fertile, well-drained soil.

Taste profile: The blossom doesn't smell as great as it looks, but adds a fantastic color to cherry blossom syrup/soda.

Health benefits: Antibacterial properties.

Store-bought alternative: None

Suggested recipes: Cherry Blossom and Flowering Currant Cordial (see page 70), Wild Sour Cherry and Flowering Currant Soda (see page 80)

Rosa
ROSE

Of particular note in this genus is dog rose (*Rosa canina*), a vigorous, arching, deciduous shrub with mid-green foliage and pale pink or white flowers, 2in (5cm) across, in early summer. The flowers, either solitary or in small clusters, are followed by masses of small, red rosehips.

Where to grow: Tolerant of poor soil but, for the best results, grow in full sun with moderately fertile, humus-rich, moist but well-drained soil.

Taste profile: Floral

Health benefits: Rosehips are the best source of vitamin C, but rose petals have significant quantities too, which makes them a great immune booster to ward off or fight a cold. The vitamin A in rose petals and

hips supports skin cells against the free radicals that cause signs of skin aging. The scent alone has a relaxing and calming effect. The antioxidants in rose-petal tea can help soothe a sore throat, while the hips have antibacterial properties, too.

Store-bought alternatives: Plenty of commercial roses available

Suggested recipe: Wild Cherry, Rose, and Cacao Nib Vodka (see page 47)

Rosmarinus
ROSEMARY

This evergreen shrub with aromatic leaves was originally cultivated on the shores of the Mediterranean.

Where to grow: Loves poor, sandy soil and full sun. Can survive on just the salt spray at the coast.

Taste profile: Piney flavor mixed with mint and sage, plus a bitter, woody aftertaste. Teas made with the fresh or dried leaves hold their flavor well.

Health benefits: Has strong effects as a memory booster. Powerful antioxidant properties, too. Inhibits the breakdown of acetylcholine, an important compound in maintaining memory and reasoning in the brain. Rosemary also increases blood flow to the brain. Has strong antibacterial, anti-inflammatory, and antiviral properties. Many claim it is also potently anticarcinogenic. The leaves are usually used, but the oils extracted from the flowers are also very potent.

Store-bought alternatives: Plenty available

Suggested recipe: Citrus Amaro (see page 87)

rose

Rumex scutatus
FRENCH OR BUCKLER LEAF SORREL

This fully hardy perennial, from Europe, North Africa, and Southwest Asia, has small, insignificant, green flowers in summer. The squat, shield-shaped, green leaves taste similar to green apples.

Where to grow: Prefers rich, damp, loamy, acid soils.

Taste profile: The most citrus-like of all the sorrel flavors and tastes the most of lemons—a great-tasting, sharp sourness. Also has the most beautiful seedpods, which taste incredible. They look like little orangey planets—they are beautiful and also taste very lemony.

Health benefits: High vitamin C content. Used for improving and cleansing the blood (like spinach) by improving the hemoglobin content.

Store-bought alternative: None

Suggested recipe: The Rockpool (see page 156)

lilac

Salvia officinalis
SAGE

From the Mediterranean and North Africa, this fully hardy perennial evergreen has woody stems, grayish leaves, and blue to purplish flowers.

Where to grow: Requires full sun and good drainage.

Taste profile: Fragrant aroma and astringent, but warm, flavor.

Health benefits: *Salvia* means "to save" or "to heal"—it has one of the longest histories of any culinary or medical herb. Particularly noted for strengthening the nervous system, improving memory, and sharpening the senses. Sage tea can be used to treat fevers and infections, as well as to ease digestive disorders. The rosmarinic acid in sage contributes to its anti-inflammatory properties.

Store-bought alternatives: Plenty available

Suggested recipe: Wild Dry Vermouth (see page 55)

Salvia elegans
PINEAPPLE SAGE

A bushy shrub with strongly pineapple-scented leaves and gorgeous, tubular, scarlet flowers on short spikes. Native to Mexico and Guatemala.

Where to grow: Grows happily in temperate climates in sheltered spots with full sun and good drainage. (The pineapple sage in the London roof garden at Midnight Apothecary flowers from late spring until the following winter.)

Taste profile: Leaves have a pineapple and herbaceous aroma and taste when used fresh as a garnish. The dried leaves produce a stronger flavor in syrups. The scarlet flowers have a pleasantly fruity, piquant, almost minty, flavor.

Health benefits: The leaves are great used fresh in a tea to treat anxiety, depression, mental fatigue, stomach acid, digestive problems, and high blood pressure. They also have cooling properties.

Store-bought alternatives: Pineapple or mint

Suggested recipes: Pineapple Sage and Scented Geranium Tea (see page 96), Bonfire of the Vani-Teas (see page 105)

Salvia microphylla
BLACKCURRANT SAGE

An evergreen member of the sage family that is native to Arizona and Mexico. It has beautiful, blackcurrant-scented leaves and striking cerise flowers.

Where to grow: Full sun and moist, well-drained soil.

Taste profile: Strong scent and taste of blackcurrant from the leaves; the flowers just look good!

Health benefits: An infusion of the leaves and flowers is traditionally used to treat fevers.

Store-bought alternative: Blackcurrants

Suggested recipes: Blackcurrant Sage, Winter Savory, and Lemon Verbena Tea (see page 97). A flowering sprig also makes a great garnish (see Beet, Cacao Nib, and Yacón Syrup Mocktail, page 136).

Syringa vulgaris
LILAC

Spring-flowering woody shrub or small tree covered in panicles of heavily fragrant blossom that is usually purple or mauve, but can also be white or pink. Native to the Balkan Peninsula.

Where to grow: Enjoys temperate climates in full sun or partial shade and moist, well-drained soil.

Taste profile: An intoxicatingly floral and sweet scent and taste when used in syrups and teas. The raw lilac blossoms are bitter, floral, and astringent.

Health benefits: Calming and relaxing. Once used to prevent recurrences of malaria.

Store-bought alternative: None

Suggested recipe: Lilac and Nettle Mocktail (see page 146)

Thymus vulgaris
THYME

A highly fragrant herb, from the western Mediterranean, with dark green leaves and mauve flowers.

Where to grow: Requires full sun and good drainage.

Taste profile: Bitter, floral, herbaceous, and piney.

Health benefits: Antimicrobial, astringent, and antiviral. The volatile oils in thyme are used to treat skin infections and urinary infections. Thyme acts as an expectorant, so is useful for coughs and colds when mucus is present. Chew the fresh leaves to relieve toothache.

Store-bought alternatives: Plenty available

Suggested recipes: Kumquat, Thyme, Cinnamon, and Honey Syrup (see page 72), Thyme and Licorice Syrup (see page 73)

Tropaeolum majus
NASTURTIUM

A sprawling annual, from Bolivia to Colombia, with bright orange/red/yellow flowers and circular green leaves with star-shaped veins.

Where to grow: Thrives in poor, well-drained soil in full sun.

Taste profile: Mustard and pepper in both the leaves and flowers.

Health benefits: Remarkable antimicrobial benefits when the fresh leaves are used in teas or tinctures due to the presence of glucosinolates—which produce pungent mustard oils when the

plant is chewed or cut—and also an antibiotic substance, flavonoids, carotenoids, and vitamin C.

Store-bought alternative: Mustard leaves

Suggested recipes: As a garnish in Beet, Cacao Nib, and Yacón Syrup Mocktail (see page 136) and Regal Mary Mocktail (see page 148)

Zanthoxylum piperitum
SZECHUAN PEPPER

An aromatic deciduous shrub originating from parts of the Far East. In spring, Szechuan pepper blooms with clusters of yellow/green flowers. The green berries, with a large, black, single seed, turn scarlet in the fall (autumn) and then burst or split open to release the seed. Branches have pairs of long, sharp thorns.

Where to grow: Easily grown in loamy soils in most positions, but prefers a good, deep, well-drained, moisture-retentive soil in full sun or partial shade.

Taste profile: Only the hull (outer shell) is used. It is intense, citrus-aromatic, and slightly floral, and leaves a tingly sensation on the lips and tongue.

Health benefits: Rich in minerals, vitamins, and antioxidants. Stimulates the appetite, supports the digestive system, and relieves toothache.

Store-bought alternative: None—it has a unique flavor.

Suggested recipes: Quince Vodka with Szechuan Pepper, Star Anise, and Juniper Berries (see page 52), Roast Quince, Szechuan Pepper, Juniper Berry, and Star Anise Mocktail (see page 138)

FEATURED FORAGER: JEKKA MCVICAR

A quick search online for Jekka McVicar makes it abundantly clear why Jekka is my horticultural hero. Although not, strictly speaking, a forager, Jekka is an organic gardening expert, author, and broadcaster. She is affectionately known as the "Queen of Herbs." Jekka cultivates wild plants in a spectacular fashion for culinary, medicinal, and ornamental uses. She very kindly invited me down to her Herboretum, near Bristol, in the U.K., and picked me some lemongrass, winter savory, and Szechuan pepper. I used these wonderful ingredients in Quince Vodka with Szechuan Pepper, Star Anise, and Juniper Berries (see page 52), Blackcurrant Sage, Winter Savory, and Lemon Verbena Tea (see page 97), and Lemongrass, Pineapple Weed, and Szechuan Teagroni (see page 108). It's a shame we don't have smell'o'vision so I can convey the sensory joy of these ingredients. Hopefully, the recipes in the book will inspire you to try them in your drinks, just as I was inspired by Jekka's enthusiasm for them.

nasturtium

PLANTS FROM THE WILD: FORAGING FOR LUXURY

Not only is wild food packed with nutrients and unique flavors, it's also great fun to find, learn about, and savor in a variety of mocktails and cocktails. The other great joy of foraging for plants is that you get to know them intimately. Indeed, as you follow them through the seasons, you'll notice changes in their shape and flavor profile (and in how they can be used), from the first signs of spring shoots packed with nutrients to cleanse and rejuvenate (see the Iced Spring Tonic Tea, on page 100) to the delicious buds and then beautiful blossoms and pollen for flavoring and garnishes. By the time many plants reach the seed stage they often pack an herbaceous or spicy punch that is ideal for alcohol infusions, bitters, and teas. You can also use some of their roots both for medicinal decoctions and as bitter flavorings in bitters, vermouth, and other infusions.

Here are some suggested plants for using in delicious drinks that are based very much on the pleasure principle for your cocktail hour.

FORAGING SAFELY

The old foraging adage: "If in doubt, leave it OUT" really does apply. Having a good field guidebook, going on guided foraging walks, and cross-referencing with other online identification sources and enthusiasts will help build your confidence as a budding forager. And don't forget to find out about the local laws and guidelines on foraging where you live. Always forage in an area free of dog walkers and never in a cemetery (where there may be arsenic waste).

Acer saccharum
SUGAR MAPLE

A species of maple tree best known for its bright red foliage in the fall (autumn) and for being the primary source of maple syrup.

Where found: Native to the hardwood forests of eastern Canada, but grows happily in cooler climates on the west coast of Canada and the U.S. and in the U.K., continental Europe, and parts of New Zealand.

Taste profile: Maple syrup ranges from a very light sweetness to caramel to a dark, bitter, burnt taste.

Health benefits: Maple syrup contains calcium, iron, magnesium, phosphorus, sodium, potassium, and zinc. Vitamins such as thiamin, riboflavin, niacin, and B6 are also found. Because maple syrup supplies inflammation-reducing polyphenol antioxidants, it can be used as part of a healthy diet in preventing diseases such as arthritis, inflammatory bowel disease, and heart disease. Maple syrup's plant-based compounds reduce oxidative stress, which speeds up the rate of aging and reduces the strength of our immune systems.

Store-bought alternatives: Plenty available

Suggested recipes: Roast Quince, Szechuan Pepper, Juniper, and Star Anise Mocktail (see page 138), Lilac and Nettle Mocktail (see page 146), Quince Delight (see page 160)

Artemesia vulgaris
MUGWORT

This member of the daisy family is native to Europe, Africa, and temperate Asia, and has naturalized in North America and New Zealand.

It can reach up to 6ft (1.8m) in height and has yellow or reddish brown flowers in summer. The leaves are toothed and dark green, with a white, silvery fuzz on the underside. Has a sage-like smell.

Where found: Waste ground, woodland edges, river banks. Mid-summer is when it really takes off.

Taste profile: The leaves and seeds have an earthy, bitter, sage-like taste—although are not nearly as bitter as wormwood, *Artemisia absinthium* (see page 28), but still powerful. Great used in bitters and vermouth.

Health benefits: The leaves and flower tops are collected and dried just before the plant blooms (usually in late summer), to treat disorders of the digestive tract and aid in all digestive functions. Mugwort is said to have antifungal, antibacterial, expectorative, and anti-asthmatic properties. It is considered a good herb for gastric disorders, stomach pains, and bowel complaints. It is used for poor appetite, indigestion, travel sickness, and stomach acidity.

Store-bought alternative: None

Suggested recipe: Wild Dry Vermouth (page 55)

Berberis darwinii
DARWIN'S BARBERRY

This dense, medium-sized evergreen shrub, from Chile and Patagonia, has dark, glossy green, broadly oblong, sparsely spined leaves and drooping racemes of rich orange flowers, tinged red in bud, followed by blue-black berries.

Where found: Parking lots, parks, gardens, coasts in sunny positions.

sugar maple

Taste profile: Young flowers taste like delicious, tropical/floral, sweet/sour fruit. When fully ripe, the fruit loses most of its acidity and is sweet.

Health benefits: The root bark is used as a tonic. Every other part, including the flowers, is antibacterial.

Store-bought alternative: None

Suggested recipe: As a garnish in Sea Buckthorn and Fermented Birch Sap Mocktail (see page 145)

Carpobrotus edulis
ICE PLANT

A creeping, succulent coastal plant that is native to South Africa and now an invasive plant across many coastal areas of the northern hemisphere. It has green, fleshy, finger-like leaves, similar to those of aloe, on a mat of reddish stems. Bright pink or yellow flowers, like sea anemones, are followed by fruits that some people call Hottentot figs or sea figs. These are edible—just!

Where found: Coastal cliffs/paths, gardens.

Taste profile: The leaves give off a lot of liquid similar to *Aloe vera* when juiced. The figs are edible if sweetened, though are nothing special.

Health benefits: The leaf juice is antiseptic, and can be gargled to treat throat and mouth infections. It is taken orally for dysentery, digestive troubles, and tuberculosis, and as a diuretic. Can also be applied externally to treat eczema, wounds, and burns. It is said to be effective against toothache and earache. Mothers used to wipe their baby's mouths after lactation with a cloth soaked in the juice of the sour fig.

Store-bought alternative: None
Suggested recipe: The Rockpool (see page 156)

Crataegus monogyna
HAWTHORN

A small, rounded deciduous tree with glossy, deeply lobed leaves, spiny branches, and sprays of cream flowers, followed by dark red berries in the fall (autumn).

Where found: Native to the U.K. and Europe, but also naturalized in the U.S. and Canada. Often used as a hedging plant, but can also be found growing as a tree in the wild. Prefers full sun.

Taste profile: Young leaves taste nutty; berries taste like overripe apples.

Health benefits: The leaves and berries are rich in the B vitamins and vitamin C. They are also packed with antioxidants that help prevent the buildup of plaques in the blood vessels supplying oxygen to the heart. Has therefore been used to promote the health of the cardiovascular system. Has also been used to reduce cholesterol. And aids digestion!

Store-bought alternative: None
Suggested recipe: Tonic Syrup (see Liz's Wild Tonics, on page 167)

Filipendula ulmaria
MEADOWSWEET

A mid-summer-flowering perennial herb with clouds of creamy, fluffy blossom that smells of almonds, honey, and vanilla. It is native to most of Europe and western Asia, but has naturalized in North America and New Zealand.

Where found: Damp meadows and marshes.

Taste profile: This aromatic plant is high in essential oils, which gives it a strong, heady scent. Young meadowsweet buds taste of pure marzipan when chewed raw. The dried leaves smell like hay, because they contain coumarin (dry the leaves quickly to avoid creating a mold that can turn the coumarin into a toxic compound). Meadowsweet is also astringent and contains a significant amount of tannins.

Health benefits: A cooling, aromatic, and astringent herb that relieves pain. The whole plant is a traditional

remedy for an acidic stomach. The most notable chemical constituent found in meadowsweet is salicylic acid, which is known to decrease pain and was the original botanical source of aspirin. A small section of root, peeled and crushed, smells like antiseptic cream and, when chewed, is a good natural remedy for relieving headaches.

Store-bought alternative: Orgeat syrup (for an almond taste)

Suggested recipes: Oaked Vodka (see page 48), Strawberry, Clover, and Meadowsweet Shrub (see page 84), Tonic Syrup (see Liz's Wild Tonics, on page 167)

Foeniculum vulgare
WILD FENNEL

A tall, hardy perennial, native to Europe, with striking, feathery, green leaves and yellow flowers in large umbels in late summer. The flowers are followed by delicious, aniseed-scented seeds in the fall (autumn).

Where found: Grows wild in Europe and most temperate countries, and is naturalized in western U.S. Likes full sun and fertile, well-drained soil.

Taste profile: The leaves have a perfume-y, anise-like flavor, while fennel pollen has a concentrated floral, citrus, and sweet-anise flavor. The seeds have a woodsy, earthy, anise flavor.

Health benefits: Aids digestion and prevents heartburn and constipation. Also has anti-inflammatory properties.

Store-bought alternative: None
Suggested recipes: Fennel Vodka (see pages 50–51), Wild Dry Vermouth (see page 55), Wild Homemade Aquavit (see page 64)

meadowsweet bud

Galium odoratum
SWEET WOODRUFF

A creeping woodland perennial, native to Europe and North Africa, with small, white flowers in spring and early summer. Narrow, bright green leaves grow beneath the flowers in successive, star-like whorls, just like cleavers or goose grass—about eight leaves to every whorl.

Where found: Woods, shaded hedgerow banks.

Taste profile: Due to the presence of coumarin, the scent and flavor when dried is like warm, newly mown hay.

Health benefits: A calmative herb for depression, insomnia, and restlessness. Improves appetite; relieves stomach pain.

Store-bought alternative: None

Suggested recipes: Cherry and Cacao Liquore (see page 90) and as a garnish in Wild Vermouth and Fermented Birch Sap Cocktail (see page 155)

Geum urbanum
HERB BENNET, WOOD AVENS, CLOVE ROOT

A perennial herb native to Europe and northern Asia, but has naturalized in parts of North America. Small, yellow flowers of five petals appear from spring right through to late fall (autumn), and occasionally beyond. The rhizomes are hard and rough, with many light brown, fibrous roots.

Where found: Favors shady places beside tree-lined country lanes, the edges of woodland, and drier land near the margins of well-shaded ponds and lakes. Likes area of disturbed soil.

Taste profile: Roots taste of cloves.

Health benefits: Use the root against diarrhea and other digestive problems. It also helps against inflammations of the mouth.

Store-bought alternative: Cloves

Suggested recipes: Wild Dry Vermouth (see page 55), Wild Homemade Aquavit (see page 64)

Heracleum sphondylium
COMMON HOGWEED

Hogweed is an herbaceous perennial or sometimes biennial, native to Europe and Asia. It has hairy, serrated leaves divided into three- to five-lobed segments. The white, sometimes pinkish, flowers each has five petals. They are arranged in large umbels, up to 8in (20cm) in diameter.

Where found: Hedgerows, woodland edges, verges, waste ground, wild gardens, from early spring to early fall (autumn). Sets seed all year round.

Taste profile: The flat, round seedpods taste like Christmas—cardamon, ginger, and orange peel—the sooner you get to them, the more pungent they are, although they still pack a punch stored. The green seeds taste more of fresh cardamon.

Health benefits: The young shoots are high in vitamin C, but it's the seeds that are claimed to be one of the strongest hormonal stimulants and sexual tonics in the world of flora. They are also thought to help regulate the activity of the nervous system, boost kidney function, and combat high blood pressure.

Store-bought alternatives: Cardamon, ginger, orange peel

Suggested recipes: Wild Dry Vermouth (see page 55), Wild Homemade Aquavit (see page 64)

sweet woodruff

Caution: Please do NOT confuse common hogweed (*Heracleum sphondylium*) with giant hogweed (*Heracleum mantegazzianum*), which is very phototoxic and should not be touched under any circumstances—it causes severe burns and blistering. Like common hogweed, giant hogweed is a member of the carrot family (*Apiaceae*), which also includes similar-looking, but highly toxic plants, such as hemlock (*Conium maculatum*).

Please be absolutely sure of the correct identification of common hogweed before foraging/using.

Juniperus
JUNIPER

Juniper is a species of conifer with needle-like leaves and seed cones. It is most commonly used as a key flavoring in gin (and Scandinavian ales). The medicinal and flavorsome parts of juniper are known as berries, but these are, in fact, dark blue-black scales from the cones.

mahonia

Where found: Grows wild throughout most parts of the cool, temperate northern hemisphere. Prefers exposed locations.

Taste profile: Astringent turpentine smell and bitter taste. Delicious!

Health benefits: The natural antibacterial, antiviral, diuretic, and antiseptic properties of juniper have been used as a treatment against infectious diseases, as well as an aid in childbirth. Extracts and essential oils from the juniper berries/scales contain a compound that stimulates the kidneys and acts as a diuretic. Amentoflavone, another compound, has antiviral properties. Juniper essential oils are also beneficial when inhaled, to treat bronchitis and to numb pain.

Store-bought alternative: Available commercially

Suggested recipes: Quince Vodka, with Szechuan Pepper, Star Anise, and Juniper Berries (see page 52), Roast Quince, Szechuan Pepper, Juniper, and Star Anise Mocktail (see page 138)

Mahonia aquifolium
OREGON GRAPE

This shade-loving evergreen shrub has large clusters of yellow flowers in spring, followed by amazing blue/purple berries that resemble grapes in the fall (autumn). *M. japonica* (Japanese mahonia) is also evergreen, with sprays of fragrant, light yellow flowers and blue/black berries.

Where found: *M. aquifolium* originates from western North America and is most often found in the understory of evergreen forests and in mountainous brushlands. In the U.K., it is a standard plant in municipal planting schemes such as grocery-store parking lots or other planting schemes for shade.

Taste profile: The berries taste very sharp and need some sort of sweetening. The flowers are ridiculously delicious eaten raw when young—sweet/sour, almost like honey with a citrus tang—and with an exquisite scent. The perfect garnish.

Health benefits: Boosts a sluggish liver, aids digestion, and is useful in balancing gut bacteria.

Store-bought alternative: None

Suggested recipes: Spring Tonic Vinegar (see page 81) and as a garnish in Iced Spring Tonic Tea (see page 100)

Matricaria discoidea
PINEAPPLE WEED

A perennial herb native to most parts of the northern and southern hemispheres, including Australia and New Zealand. The leaves have a feathery, chamomile-like appearance. The flowers appear once the summer heat really gets going and are daisy-like, with white petals that do not last long. The inner yellow/green corollas are dome-shaped.

Where found: Usually in poor, compacted soil around footpaths, field entrances, waste ground, and roadsides.

Taste profile: The flowerheads smell and taste strongly of pineapple. The later in the season you pick them, the more bitter the aftertaste.

Health benefits: Has been used to treat gastrointestinal upset, sores, and fevers. Also a mild sedative like its relative, chamomile.

Store-bought alternative: None

Suggested recipes: Wild Dry Vermouth (see page 55), Lemongrass, Pineapple Weed, and Szechuan Teagroni (see page 108), Virgin and Vegan Piña Colada (see page 140)

Mertensia maritima
OYSTER LEAF, OYSTERPLANT

A creeping perennial herb (in the same family as borage) that is native to the coasts of northern and western Scotland, Canada, and Greenland. The trailing stems bear succulent, blue-green leaves with an oyster-like flavor. Bright blue and pink flowers appear from early to late summer. The Scots' Gaelic name means "gift of the sea."

Where found: Grows on gravely ground and shingle by the sea in the northern hemisphere, but is quite rare.

Taste profile: Salt, mushrooms, minerality—it has the brininess and earthiness of oysters!

Health benefits: Rich in zinc, manganese, potassium, and iron. Also has antioxidant properties beneficial for improving skin, immunity, and memory.

Store-bought alternative: None

Suggested recipe: The Rockpool (page 156)

Oxalis articulata
PINK SORREL

A perennial native to parts of South America that has naturalized throughout Europe, North America, North Africa, and northern and western Asia. It has three-lobed leaves with heart-shaped leaflets—a bit like a shamrock—and delicate, pink flowers.

Where found: Bare and disturbed ground, often close to areas of habitation by the edges of woods.

Taste profile: Delicious lemony/apple-y, acidic taste.

Health benefits: Contains vitamin B-complex, vitamin C, and calcium. Helps reduce fevers and quenches the thirst.

Store-bought alternative: None

Suggested recipe: Iced Spring Tonic Tea (see page 100)

Palmaria palmata
DULSE

One of the red seaweeds, this is reddish brown to deep reddish/purple in color, and leathery in texture. The flat fronds can grow up to 20in (50cm) long.

Where found: Grows on rocks on the middle to lower shore of North Atlantic and Pacific coasts (likes cold water).

Taste profile: Savory, umami, salty, bacon (when fried!).

Health benefits: Seaweeds are more easily digested and contain more vitamins, nutrients, and minerals weight-for-weight than land plants.

Dulse is a good source of vitamins and minerals. It contains all the trace elements needed by humans and has high levels of protein and iron.

Store-bought alternative: Commercially available in dried form

Suggested recipe: The Rockpool (see page 156)

Primula vulgaris
PRIMROSE

A perennial forming a rosette of tongue-shaped leaves, with many scented, usually primrose-yellow flowers in early spring.

Where found: Partial shade in woodland and hedgerows, and on verges.

Taste profile: Sweet, slightly apple-y flowers.

Health benefits: The leaves, flowers, and root make a mild sedative in an infusion.

Store-bought alternative: None

Suggested recipes: Spring Tonic Vinegar (see page 81), Iced Spring Tonic Tea (see page 100)

Prunus avium
SWEET CHERRY

or *Prunus cerasus* (sour cherry)

Small deciduous tree with small, rich, fleshy fruit in late summer with a pitt (stone) in the middle. The fruits are usually dark red, but can also be pale pink or even yellow. Sour cherries are more acidic and bitter.

Where found: Parks, gardens, woodland, streets in any temperate climate.

Taste profile: Sweet (and tart if you are using *Prunus cerasus*).

pink sorrel

Health benefits: The anthocyanins (the red pigment in many fruits) are packed with antioxidants and have been shown to lower cholesterol. One study showed that drinking a glass of cherry juice is equivalent to eating 23 portions of vegetables a day. Cherries contain numerous vitamins, including A and C, and are high in nutrients such as beta-carotene and potassium.

Prunus serrulata
JAPANESE CHERRY

A small deciduous tree, native to China, Japan, and Korea, with light pink flowers that hang in drooping clusters in late spring.

Where found: Parks, gardens, and streets in any temperate climate.

Taste profile: Floral and almond-y.

Health benefits: Antioxidant properties.

Store-bought alternative: None

Suggested recipes: Cherry Blossom and Flowering Currant Cordial (see page 70), Magnolia and Cherry Blossom Shrub (see page 83), Gorse and Cherry Blossom Gimlet (see page 160)

Store-bought alternative: None

Suggested recipes: Wild Cherry, Rose, and Cacao Nib Vodka (see page 47), Cherry and Cacao Liquore (see page 90), Liquore Digestif (see page 159)

Pseudotsuga menziesii
DOUGLAS FIR

Large, fast-growing evergreen tree, conical in habit, with the bark becoming thick and rugged. The soft, dark green leaves spiral slightly around the branches.

Where found: Woodlands of western and eastern North America, parts of the U.K. and continental Europe, and parts of Australia and New Zealand.

Taste profile: Lemony, piney, tart, resinous—the aromatic volatile oils carry really well in infusions.

Health benefits: A decoction of the leaves and/or bark was used for centuries by First Nation Americans for rheumatism, as a remedy for seasonal colds, as a diuretic, and for unspecified kidney and bladder ailments. A cold infusion of the needles was used as a mouthwash. The young fresh leaf tips are rich in vitamin C and a popular spring tonic. Also great used in teas and vinegars. It has anti-inflammatory properties.

Store-bought alternative: None

Suggested recipes: Douglas Fir-infused Gin (see page 54), Douglas Fir Gin and Bee Pollen Cocktail (see page 150), Into the Woods (see page 170)

Smyrnium olusatrum
ALEXANDERS

A biennial herb, originally from the Mediterranean, which grows up to 5ft (1.5m) tall. It has bluntly toothed, flat leaves and green/yellow flowers arranged in umbels in spring, then forms near-black seeds.

Where found: Alexanders are salt-tolerant and thrive near the coast. They can also be found inland.

Taste profile: Tastes like pungent celery and parsley mixed with myrrh. The seeds make an aromatic, peppery seasoning and are great crushed into vodka to give it some oomph!

Health benefits: In the past alexanders were used to treat asthma, menstrual problems, and wounds. The chemical compounds have been found to aid digestion.

Store-bought alternatives: Celery or parsley

Suggested recipes: Homemade Tonic Water Syrup (see page 78), Iced Spring Tonic Tea (see page 100)

Stellaria media
CHICKWEED

A low-growing annual that is native to Europe, but which has naturalized in many parts of North America. Has tiny, white, star-like flowers.

Where found: In long grass or grass verges, hedgerows, and woodland. Also thrives in areas of disturbed soil. Needs moist soil. Germinates and flowers at any time of the year, but mainly in spring and fall (autumn).

Taste profile: Fresh and grassy

Health benefits: This makes a great spring tonic. Chickweed is packed with ascorbic acid, beta-carotene, calcium, magnesium, niacin, potassium, riboflavin, selenium, thiamin, zinc, copper, and gamma-linolenic acid. People take chickweed for constipation, stomach and bowel problems, blood disorders, asthma and other lung diseases, obesity, vitamin C deficiency, psoriasis, and muscle and joint pain.

Store-bought alternative: None

Suggested recipes: Spring Tonic Vinegar (see page 81), Iced Spring Tonic Tea (see page 100)

Taraxacum officinale
DANDELION

Perennial herb with a rosette of lobed, green leaves that sprout from a stout taproot. Has bright yellow flowerheads from spring to fall (autumn).

Where found: Parks, gardens, hard surfaces, lawns, roadsides, cultivated ground, garbage tips—everywhere!

Taste profile: Earthy, nutty, bitter.

Health benefits: Young dandelion leaves are one of the best bitter spring tonics for flushing out the kidneys and stoking the digestive fires. The dandelion contains more vitamin A than almost any other foraged plant. Also contains high levels of vitamins C, D, and B-complex, iron, magnesium, zinc, potassium, manganese, choline, and calcium. It is a diuretic and mild laxative. The root is traditionally used as a liver and skin remedy, as a blood tonic for fasting, and, as the root is high in inulin (a natural prebiotic for intestinal flora), it can help heal digestive issues, balance blood sugar, and moderate estrogen levels.

Douglas Fir

Store-bought alternative: None

Suggested recipes: Citrus Amaro (see page 87), Iced Spring Tonic Tea (see page 100)

Trifolium pratense
RED CLOVER

A short biennial or perennial, native to Europe and northern Asia, with blossomy flowerheads that are red, pink, or pinkish-purple.

Where found: Loves wet and dry grassland, woodland, forest margins, field borders, and paths.

Taste profile: Sweet-tasting. Needs a long infusion (20–30 minutes) to draw out the sweet and savory notes—like floral, honey-roasted vegetables!

Health benefits: Red clover is one of the richest sources of isoflavones, which are water-soluble chemicals that act like estrogens. It's thus used to relieve hot flashes (flushes) and PMS, as well as to lower cholesterol levels and improve urine production and blood circulation. It can also help prevent osteoporosis and reduce the possibility of blood clots and arterial plaques. Also a source of nutrients such as calcium, magnesium, potassium, and vitamin C.

Store-bought alternative: None

Suggested recipe: Strawberry, Clover, and Meadowsweet Shrub (see page 84)

Ulex europaeus
GORSE

An evergreen European shrub with spiny branches and bright yellow flowers, situated on the spines and either solitary or in pairs. Gorse flowers for most of the year, but peaks in mid- and late spring.

Where found: Wasteland, open moorland, heathland, highway embankments, sunny sites, sandy soil.

Taste profile: Earthy coconut!

Health benefits: High in protein. Gorse has surprisingly few medicinal uses, though the flowers have been used to treat jaundice, scarlet fever, diarrhea, and kidney stones.

Store-bought alternative: None

Suggested recipes: Gorse Rum (see page 63), Gorse and Cherry Blossom Gimlet (see page 160)

Urtica dioica
NETTLE

A perennial found in nearly every temperate climate where it receives plentiful sunlight. Appears in early spring, but new growth often occurs again in the fall (autumn).

Where found: Damp areas or where land has been disturbed by humans. Needs plenty of sun and moisture.

Taste profile: Similar to spinach.

Health benefits: Nettle leaves, seeds, and roots are a nutritional powerhouse, providing high levels of calcium, magnesium, iron, and potassium, among other nutrients. Nettle contains vitamins C, D, and K, and B-complex. Its blood-invigorating properties make it a great spring tonic, but use the young nettle tops, not the older, darker leaves. Its key uses are cleansing and detoxification. The leaves and roots have been used to treat allergy symptoms (i.e. those of hayfever). Nettles contain compounds that reduce inflammation and can treat arthritis, rheumatism, and high blood pressure. The seeds make a great garnish—thanks Liz Knight (see *Featured Foragers*, on page 166) for that tip! These are mineral-rich, great for the skin and

violets

hair, and for supporting the urinary system. The leaves are gentler, while the seeds pack more of a punch.

Store-bought alternative: None

Suggested recipes: Iced Spring Tonic Tea (see page 100), Liz's Wild Tonics (see page 167)

Viola
VIOLETS

An early-spring, sweet-scented perennial herb native to Europe, the Middle East, and North Africa, but now naturalized in other cooler parts of the northern hemisphere.

Where found: Woodland, shaded hedgerows.

Taste profile: Sweet, floral.

Health benefits: Used as a cough remedy and anti-inflammatory, particularly for bronchitis and for rheumatic complaints using the root. The flowers are slightly sedative and good for treating insomnia.

Store-bought alternative: None

Suggested recipes: Iced Spring Tonic Tea (see page 100), Violet Tea (see page 101)

CHAPTER 3
ALCOHOL INFUSIONS

Making an infusion simply describes the process of extracting the flavor, color, vitamins, and other elements of flowers, leaves, citrus peel, and so on, into a solvent such as alcohol, water, oil, or vinegar. All the infusions in this chapter use alcohol as the solvent and exploit wonderfully floral, aromatic, and/or bitter ingredients to provide your taste buds with enough interest that they don't crave sweet sensations. Often the base alcohol, herbs, or fruit will have enough sweetness to do the job. If you wish to incorporate additional sweetness, that's entirely up to you when you're building your mocktails or cocktails. However, this method keeps your options open.

All these infusions can stand alone, only requiring some ice and possibly dilution in the form of sparkling or tonic water. You can also add a splash of vermouth to provide another layer of aromatics and flavor.

SUCCESSFUL INFUSING

There are many different ways to infuse plant material, but following a few simple guidelines will guarantee success. I suggest using a high-proof/alcohol by volume (ABV)—80 proof/40% ABV (or higher)—spirit where possible. This will extract the maximum amount of flavor and herbal alkaloids from your ingredients. The high-alcohol content also acts as a preservative and so increases the shelf life of the infusion. I recommend starting your infusion experiments with vodka, because it has a neutral taste, and before you try other flavor combinations.

The trick with putting any fresh vegetal matter in a bottle is to do so for the least amount of time—you don't want the bitter, vegetal taste as the chlorophyll breaks down. So it's best to put lots in for the shortest period of time. As soon as green matter loses its color (turning from vibrant green to dull gray), it's usually time to take it out. Straining is also important. Using pieces of muslin/cheesecloth or a coffee filter (I use an AeroPress®) is key to removing those really tiny particles that can have an adverse effect on taste over time.

When working out how long to leave the plant material to infuse, it is best to err on the side of caution. Although it is great to experiment, I suggest tasting your infusions regularly to check you haven't left them for too long. The following is intended as a general guide to infusion times:

- Strong flavors such as lavender or vanilla beans (pods): a couple of hours to a day
- Fresh herbs, pine needles, citrus zest, fresh ginger: a maximum of 1 to 3 days
- Most berries, stone fruits: 3 days to 1 week
- Vegetables, apples, and pears: 5 to 7 days
- Dried spices and really mild flavors: up to 2 weeks

I have provided the quantities of plant material you will need for each recipe, but, as a rule-of-thumb, aim for the following ratios with your chosen spirit:

- Fresh herbs, pine needles, citrus zest, fresh ginger: 1:4 ingredient to spirit
- Berries, fruits, stone fruits: 1:1 ingredient to spirit
- Dried herbs: 1:8 ingredient to spirit
- Dried spices: 1:10 ingredient to spirit

CITRIC ACID

I have started using citric acid in my infusions to provide a level of mellow acidity, which means you don't usually need to add any further citrus to your cocktails. The sterilizing qualities of citric acid also increase the shelf life of the infusion. If you use lemon or other citrus juices instead, this can make the whole infusion go cloudy and you risk it going off over time. However, the skins of citrus fruit, freed of their bitter white pith, provide the fabulous citrus, bitter flavor you want, so keep adding them.

Wild Cherry, Rose, and Cacao Nib VODKA

This is a grown-up infusion that sounds quite sweet, but is actually pretty bitter and sharp, with enough floral and fruity goings-on to keep you satisfied. Cherries, chocolate, and roses go very well together and where there are cherries growing in the wild, chances are there will also be wild roses—either the delicate dog rose (*Rosa canina*) or the more brightly colored and flavored *Rosa rugosa*—growing close by. I've suggested using sour cherries (*Prunus cerasus*) here, as they add a wonderful sharpness to the infusion. They need about a week to extract their flavor properly, as do the roses. The cacao nibs, however, will be more or less done after three days (although you can leave them for a week and so add them at the same time as the cherries and roses).

2 large handfuls of fresh, wild, unsprayed rose petals

1lb (450g) fresh sour cherries or ½lb (225g) frozen sour cherries

3oz (90g) roasted cacao nibs

700 or 750ml bottle of vodka, 80 proof/40% ABV

1-quart (1-liter) wide-mouthed, sealable jar, sterilized (see page 24)

Fine-mesh strainer and muslin/cheesecloth or gold coffee filter (see page 20)

Sealable presentation bottle(s), sterilized (see page 24)

Makes approximately 1 quart (1 liter)

Pick the rose petals on the morning of a hot day, after the dew has lifted but before the sun has zapped a lot of their essential oils. Remove the pits (stones) from the cherries, chop into small pieces, and add them to the sterilized jar. Add the pits to the jar, too. (If you are using frozen cherries, allow them to thaw thoroughly before adding them to the jar.)

Add the rose petals and roasted cacao nibs to the jar, pour in the vodka, and seal tightly. Upend the jar a couple of times and store in a cool, dark place for 5 days. Fine-strain the infusion (see page 25) into a wide-mouthed pitcher, then funnel into the sterilized presentation bottle(s). The resulting infusion will be dry, tart, and very grown up.

VARIATION

This recipe (minus the cacao nibs) can be used for any kind of fruit that is not too sweet. Try substituting the cherries for blackcurrants, red currants, or wild blueberries, for example. You could also change the base spirit to grappa or aged brandy.

Cacao nibs are essentially raw chocolate—pieces of cacao beans that have been roasted, hulled, and prepared before the stage of actually making chocolate. They taste slightly more of roasted coffee beans, although there are very detectable chocolate notes.

Oaked VODKA

This infusion imitates the soaking and heat treatment of the oak barrels used to age Scotch whisky. I used vodka in this recipe because I wanted a very versatile "aged" spirit that would pair with a variety of ingredients. I wouldn't dream of spoiling a decent whisky, but if you have a young, unaged whisky, try this method by all means.

There are two methods for oak-aging the vodka: a cheat's way that produces reasonable results in a month and a longer method which takes up to six months, but has more impressive results. I did try a method using charred oak sticks (available online), which was supposed to be effective in 24 hours, but found the results disappointing. My shortcut version uses ready-prepared, pharmaceutical oak bark chips and doesn't involve charring the wood (which is essential in an authentic, barrel-aged version).

By adding the other botanical ingredients you are imitating the notes that develop over a longer time in a barrel as the charred wood reacts with the ethanol. Without them, the solitary taste of oak would be unbalanced. In addition, the dried tutsan (*Hypericum androsaemum*) provides a lovely amber scent. I have suggested using foraged or garden ingredients, but where possible also provided commercially available alternatives in brackets. Try using Oaked Vodka in Into The Woods (see page 170).

1-quart (1-liter) wide-mouthed, sealable jar, sterilized (see page 24)

Fine-mesh strainer and muslin/cheesecloth or coffee filter (see page 20)

Sealable presentation bottle(s), sterilized (see page 24)

Makes approximately 1 quart (1 liter)

2 tsp pharmaceutical-standard oak bark chips (or apple or cherry wood)

Large handful of herb bennet (*Geum urbanum*) roots, washed and finely chopped (or 3 cloves)

10 hogweed (*Heracleum sphondylium*) seeds, green or dried (or 3 allspice berries)

1 tbsp dried tutsan leaves and flowers

1 tbsp dried marjoram leaves

1 tbsp dried meadowsweet (*Filipendula ulmaria*) seeds (or 1 vanilla bean/pod)

2 tsp (10ml) raw runny honey

1 liter bottle of vodka, 80 proof/40% ABV minimum, preferably stronger

SHORT METHOD:

Add all the dry ingredients and honey to the sterilized jar. Pour in the vodka, stir, and seal. Infuse for 2 weeks in a dark place at room temperature. Shake and taste occasionally.

When you're happy with the results, fine-strain the infusion (see page 25) into a wide-mouthed pitcher, then funnel into the sterilized presentation bottle(s) and seal. For extra clarity when straining the infusion, use an AeroPress® filter.

Allow the strained infusion to stand for another 2 weeks, to allow the flavors to mellow and "mature." Store in a cool, dark place and consume within 6 months.

herb bennet root

LONG METHOD:

2oz (60g) pharmaceutical-standard oak bark chips (or apple or cherry wood)

1 liter bottle of vodka, 80 proof/40% ABV minimum, preferably stronger

For the longer version, I suggest you also buy specially prepared woodchips, because normal oak bark needs a lot of soaking, boiling, re-soaking, and baking to free it of the hardening agents that would otherwise spoil the taste of the long-term infusion. This longer method doesn't require the additional botanical ingredients.

Preheat the oven to 350°F/180°C/Gas 4. Place about 2oz (60g) of the prepared woodchips on a baking sheet and bake them in the oven. Check the woodchips every 15 minutes or so. A light burning (when smoke first appears) provides vanilla, fruity overtones. A medium burning (when there's smoke and smell) provides almond, coconut, caramel, and spicy notes. A strong burning (when the wood changes color) provides smoky chocolate tones. A medium burning will take around 1 hour. Don't burn the chips completely. Once the woodchips are ready, boil them for 10 minutes in a saucepan of water, to help reduce some of the tannic astringency that can come from the wood. Strain the woodchips and set aside.

Pour the vodka into the sterilized jar, add the woodchips, and seal. Leave to infuse in a cold, dark place for 3–6 months. Watch the color change and taste each week until the infusion is to your liking.

Strain as for the Short Method and, again, mature for at least 1 week in a cool, dark place before drinking. Consume within 6 months.

Fennel VODKA

This is beautifully simple and utterly delicious. You can use fennel blossom/stalks in summer and fennel seeds in late summer/fall. This plant is so abundant in our garden and to be found all over local parks and marshes—in fact, in most urban areas. The fennel of which I speak is wild fennel (*Foeniculum vulgare*), as opposed to Florence fennel (*F. vulgare* var. *azoricum*), which is grown in gardens as an annual, with the whole plant being dug up for eating. (You can, however, use the bulb of Florence fennel in an infusion—the mild, warm, sweet aromatic taste of licorice just needs some homemade bitters to really make the drink complete.) Although the fennel seed infusion is great, it will not have quite the same vibrancy and intensity as one made with fennel blossom. That said, both infusions are pretty darn delicious.

Fennel blossom

FENNEL BLOSSOM VODKA

Fennel blossom is astonishingly fragrant, and also full of complex and volatile essential oils that the seeds do not carry. The chlorophyll and sweet pollen from the fresh plant will also give your infusion more color than the fennel seed.

15 heads of fennel blossom

700 or 750ml bottle of smooth vodka, 80 proof/40% ABV, such as Black Cow

3 or 4 x 10-in (25-cm) long fennel frond stalks, chopped

1-quart (1-liter) wide-mouthed, sealable jar, sterilized (see page 24)

Sealable presentation bottle(s), sterilized (see page 24)

Makes approximately 1½ pints (750ml)

Hold the heads of fennel blossom over a plate or chopping board and shake to release the pollen. Pour the vodka into the sterilized jar, then add the pollen and fennel stalks. Seal and shake the jar, then store in a cool, dark place for 3 days. Check daily to see if the fennel stalks have turned dull gray. If they have, remove them. Taste to see if the infusion is strong enough. If so, strain into a wide-mouthed pitcher, then funnel into the sterilized presentation bottle(s) and seal. Store in a cool, dark place and consume within 6 months.

There should still be a few heads of yellow pollen, as well as fully formed seeds, over fall/winter. You can collect and store these to provide a wonderful edible garnish for your cocktails—use either the whole head or just some fennel pollen.

If you suffer from gastro-intestinal cramp (or gas), the anethole (an aromatic compound) in fennel should smooth the muscles in your intestinal tract and relieve the discomfort. Fennel also allays hunger and was thought to be a cure for obesity in Renaissance Europe.

Fennel seed

FENNEL SEED VODKA

Fennel seeds impart a touch of sweetness, as well as their licorice flavor. Try broiling (grilling) or dry-frying the seeds first to intensify their flavor.

2 tbsp fennel seeds

700 or 750ml bottle of smooth vodka, 80 proof/40% ABV, such as Black Cow

Pestle and mortar

1-quart (1-liter) wide-mouthed, sealable jar, sterilized (see page 24)

Sealable presentation bottle(s), sterilized (see page 24)

Makes approximately 1½ pints (750ml)

Broil (grill) or dry-fry the seeds on a low heat until they begin to smell and change color. Gently crack the seeds in the pestle and mortar. Add the cracked seeds to the sterilized jar and pour in the vodka. Seal, gently shake, and leave for up to 1 week in a cool, dark place. Taste to see if the infusion is strong enough. When you are happy, strain the infusion into a wide-mouthed pitcher, funnel into the sterilized presentation bottle(s), and seal. Store in a cool, dark place and consume within 6 months.

quince

Quince VODKA

WITH SZECHUAN PEPPER, STAR ANISE, AND JUNIPER BERRIES

This recipe arose after seeing a photograph taken by my gardening hero Jekka McVicar (see *Featured Forager*, on page 35) of her Szechuan pepper (*Zanthoxylum piperitum*) harvest. The image of black seeds peeking through a red casing against an indigo autumnal sky was beautiful. Jekka later explained that you discard the seed (or keep it to grow future plants), as it is the red casing that has the amazing, floral, tingly, citrus flavor. Some people liken the experience of eating Szechuan to licking a battery, but I wanted to showcase it in an infusion. Quince (*Cydonia oblonga*) and juniper berries were also ripening, so it seemed a happy marriage. The quince is the other real star. There is a perfume-y headiness to the scent of quince when given time or heat—in this case, time in the infusion. The quince and lemon with the citric acid provide enough acidity; the Szechuan pepper, star anise, and juniper berries bring bitterness and aromatics; and the vodka provides sweet creaminess. Try this infusion in the Quince Delight cocktail (see page 160 and in glasses opposite).

700 or 750ml bottle of smooth, triple-distilled vodka, 80 proof/40% ABV minimum, such as Black Cow

7 Szechuan peppercorns

7 juniper berries

2 star anise

3 quince

4 lemon wheels

½ tsp citric acid (optional)

1-quart (1-liter) wide-mouthed, sealable jar, sterilized (see page 24)

Pestle and mortar

Sealable presentation bottle(s), sterilized (see page 24)

Makes approximately 1½ pints (750ml)

Quince brown very easily, so pour a small amount of vodka into the sterilized jar before you start adding them, to ensure they are covered at all times.

Crack the spices with the pestle and mortar to release their flavor, then drop them into the jar.

Use a cloth to rub the gray down from the quince and then rinse them. With a very sharp knife (as quince are extremely hard), carefully slice the quince, with the skin on, as finely as you can to maximize the surface area that will be exposed to the vodka. Put the slices straight into the vodka, ensuring they are never exposed to the air. Add the lemon wheels and citric acid (if using). Seal the jar, shake gently, and store somewhere cool and dark.

Remove the star anise after 24 hours (they are very potent and can overpower the other flavors), but leave the other ingredients for 2 weeks, or no longer than a month. Strain the infusion into a wide-mouthed pitcher, then funnel into the sterilized presentation bottle(s) and seal. Keep in a cool, dark place for up to 6 months. (Note: If you haven't used any citric acid, which acts as a preservative, then strain and remove the lemon slices after 7 days, and refrigerate the infusion on completion, consuming within a month.)

The mellow, almost tropical, sweetness exuded by infused quince is in direct contrast to the unapproachable astringency you experience on sinking your teeth into a raw one. It is as stark a contrast as a roaring fireside versus the harsh frozen wastes outside.

Star anise (*Illicium verum*), like quince, has a wonderful headiness, with a strong background of licorice, and somehow provides sweet, herbal, and slightly hot notes. But be warned: star anise is very potent and a small amount for a short time goes a long way—if you leave it in for too long, then you will overpower the other beautiful ingredients.

Douglas Fir-infused GIN

This is an instant infusion that provides piney, citrusy, earthy gorgeousness with a hint of astringency. I use this infusion as the base for the Douglas Fir Gin and Bee Pollen Cocktail (see page 150). Douglas fir (*Pseudotsuga menziesii*) is packed with vitamin C and electrolytes, and has my favorite scent and taste of all the firs, spruce, and larches. Douglas fir needles were used in North America by the First Nations and also by early settlers (on the former's recommendation) to get them through the winter without dying of malnutrition. I make this infusion all year round, so it's interesting to note how it changes in taste through the seasons. The lime-green new growth that emerges in spring is more tart, whereas the winter needles are more aromatic and almost bitter.

3 handfuls of Douglas fir needles

2 x 2in- (5-cm) lengths of very thin, woody Douglas fir stems

700 or 750ml bottle of gin, 80 proof/40% ABV

Food blender

1-quart (1-liter) wide-mouthed, sealable jar, sterilized (see page 24)

Fine-mesh strainer and muslin/ cheesecloth or coffee filter (see page 20)

Sealable presentation bottle(s), sterilized (see page 24)

Makes approximately 1½ pints (750ml)

Place the Douglas fir needles and woody stems in the blender, adding enough gin to cover them, and then blend for at least 30 seconds on a high speed.

Pour the bright green mix into the sterilized jar and add the remaining gin. Seal the jar, gently upend a couple of times, and it's done. The infusion can remain in this state for about 4 days, before becoming unpleasant. Fine-strain the infusion (see page 25) into a wide-mouthed pitcher, then funnel into the sterilized presentation bottle(s) and seal. Store in a cool, dark place and consume within a year.

Douglas fir is not a true fir, but simply named as such by a European botanist who visited northwest America in the 1700s. You can identify Douglas fir by its distinctive leaves. They are all the same length, pointed at the tip— although they don't hurt when you brush against them—and arranged spirally around the branch (as opposed to the flat sprays of true fir or the needle tips of spruce).

If you want to add an extra layer of perfume-y aromatics, the sticky resin on young trees often gathers in blisters under the bark. These can be "popped" with a sharp knife and added in situ directly to your cocktail mix (use about 1 teaspoon per drink) or used as a sticky aromatic rim on the glass. The resin is difficult to collect, solidifies quickly, and is not sweet at all, but it's quite impressive if you happen to be serving cocktails al fresco!

Wild
DRY VERMOUTH

Wild vermouth allows you to play around with aromatic and bitter ingredients, and pack them into an aperitif. Vermouth is, essentially, white wine fortified with hard liquor to bring it up to about 32–40 proof/16–20% ABV. This is the perfect aperitif for me: not too alcoholic, deliciously bitter-sweet balanced, and with minimal sweetener to take the edge off—but only just. You can, of course, adjust the level of sweetness, but this recipe is going to come out on the dry side.

Tincturing (see pages 56–57) some of the tougher, or more bitter and aromatic, ingredients in advance will certainly improve the blend of the final vermouth, and offer more tannic and bitter depth and complexity. However, you can infuse the other more delicately flavored ingredients on the day. The trick and the fun lie in experimenting with aromatic and bitter ingredients close at hand, whether from your garden, hedgerow, or pantry.

As with a good perfume or piece of music, make sure you have a few deep base notes (around 10–50 percent) of bitter and aromatic flavors, such as wormwood (*Artemisia absinthium*) and/or mugwort (*A. vulgaris*) or yarrow (*Achillea millefolium*), balanced with some sweeter top notes (such as fennel, mint, or fruit), and then a range of herbaceous or floral notes in the middle (like gorse, chamomile, and pineapple weed). And why not vary your vermouths according to the season? Either sip the vermouth, very chilled, on its own or use it in the Wild Negroni Cocktail (see page 153), the Douglas Fir Gin and Bee Pollen Cocktail (see page 150), or the Wild Vermouth and Fermented Birch Sap Cocktail (see page 155).

hogweed seed

sage leaves

hogweed

5 x small, sealable glass jars (as used for jellies and jams), sterilized (see page 24)

Labels, to identify the jars

Nonreactive pan

Fine-mesh strainer and muslins/ cheesecloths or coffee filters (see page 20)

Sealable presentation bottle(s), sterilized (see page 24)

Makes approximately 1 quart (1 liter)

1 heaped tbsp green hogweed (*Heracleum sphondylium*) seeds or 1 level tbsp brown hogweed seeds

¼ cup (5g) freshly chopped herb bennet (*Geum urbanum*) roots or 1 heaped tbsp dried herb bennet

¼ cup (5g) fresh wormwood or 1 heaped tbsp dried wormwood

¼ cup (5g) fresh orange zest or 1 heaped tbsp finely chopped dried orange zest

¼ cup (5g) fresh sage or 1 heaped tbsp dried sage

700 or 750ml bottle of high-proof vodka, 100 proof/50% ABV minimum, to cover the tinctured ingredients (about 5oz/150ml per tincture will be plenty)

STAGE 1

To get optimum bitterness and aromatics from your five key ingredients, I suggest tincturing the hogweed, herb bennet, wormwood, orange zest, and sage in advance. To tincture, you will need to immerse a small amount of each plant material in high-proof vodka and leave it for a few days—I have suggested about a week here, but feel free to experiment. You don't need to measure out the ingredients precisely. If you are using fresh ingredients, aim for 1 part fresh material to 2 parts alcohol (i.e. double the height). If you are using dried

orange zest

herb bennet roots

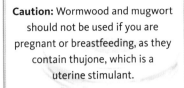

wormwood

material, use five times the amount of alcohol as plant material. You are aiming for a final yield of only 4 teaspoons (20ml) of tinctured liquid from each ingredient (and not all of that will make it into the final blend).

Chop each ingredient separately and finely to expose as much surface area to alcohol as possible and put in a separate sterilized jar (you should have a total of five jars). Cover the ingredients in the jars with the high-proof vodka and seal. Label the jars with the ingredient's name and the date, and keep in a cool, dark place for 1 week.

Aromatized and fortified wines can be traced back to India in 1500BC. Like most booze, and bitter booze in particular, these wines have medicinal origins—expelling nasties from the body, soothing inflammation, quelling stomach disorders, and aiding digestion. The bitter compounds of wormwood form the traditional base bitter for vermouth (which, incidentally, is the French pronunciation of *wermut*, the German word for "wormwood"). They are fantastic appetite stimulants, but you can play around with many additional and alternative bitter and aromatic ingredients.

¼ cup (5g) fresh yarrow leaves or 2 tsp dried yarrow

¼ cup (5g) fresh gorse (*Ulex europaeus*) flowers or 1 tbsp dried gorse

¼ cup (5g) fresh chamomile (*Chamaemelum nobile*) flowers or 1 tbsp dried chamomile

¼ cup (5g) fresh mugwort leaves or 2 tsp dried mugwort

1 heaped tbsp pineapple weed (*Matricaria discoidea*) flowers

1 tbsp Douglas fir (*Pseudotsuga menziesii*) needles

3 fresh marjoram sprigs

2 tsp wild fennel (*Foeniculum vulgare*) seeds

1 tsp black peppercorns, lightly crushed

1 tsp toasted coriander seeds

5 juniper berries

1 clove

1 cardamom pod, lightly crushed

750ml bottle of dry white wine (such as Chenin Blanc)

⅓ cup (100ml) grappa or other unaged brandy

2 tbsp (30ml) raw honey

STAGE 2

After 1 week fine-strain each of the tinctures (see page 25) separately and funnel the clear liquids into separate clean jars. Put on the lids and store in a cool, dark place until ready to use.

Add all the Stage 2 plant material and spices to a nonreactive saucepan, pour in the wine and grappa (or a brandy of your choice), and warm over a medium heat until bubbles start to rise. Do not allow the wine to boil. Add the honey and stir to dissolve. The honey will help draw out the flavors of the botanicals. Allow the mix to cool and infuse overnight.

juniper berries

STAGE 3

Fine-strain the infused wine and honey into a wide-mouthed pitcher. You should have about 2 cups (500ml) of wine (some of the original 3 cups/750ml of wine will have been absorbed by the solid ingredients and/or evaporated).

You now need to add the tinctured ingredients. For every 2 cups (500ml) of wine, you need to add approximately ⅔ cup (150ml) of hard liquor (some or all of which will come from your tinctures). Using a tablespoon (15ml) and teaspoon (5ml), I suggest pouring in 1 tablespoon (15ml) each of the hogweed, herb bennet, and sage tinctures; 2 tablespoons (30ml) of the orange-peel tincture; and 1 teaspoon (5ml) of the wormwood tincture.

Stir the mix and taste. If you think it needs more bitterness, add another teaspoon of the wormwood, but go steady, as it's very bitter. Feel free to adjust the quantities and play around until you are pleased with the results. If you have only used about 5 tablespoons (80ml) of your tinctured ingredients, you will need to top up the vermouth with grappa (or your other chosen liquor) to reach 5oz (150ml) of liquor.

Finally, fine-strain the vermouth one more time into a clean, wide-mouthed pitcher, using either two layers of rinsed muslin/cheesecloth or coffee filters. Repeat if necessary. Funnel the vermouth into the sterilized presentation bottle(s), seal, and refrigerate. Wait at least 24 hours before drinking the vermouth, to let the flavors fully meld. Use your vermouth within 2 months, storing it in the refrigerator between uses, as it will start to oxidize as soon as you expose it to air.

BASIL-INFUSED
Dolin Blanc Vermouth

If your ardor for homemade drinks doesn't extend to making your own vermouths, you can still add some herbaceousness to store-bought varieties in the same way that you would infuse hard liquor. The trick is to be mindful of the existing and complex botanicals that will already have been carefully chosen for a good-quality vermouth. The flavor of basil (*Ocimum basilicum*) is closely associated with Italy; it will complement the aromatized wine and pair nicely with food you might nibble on when drinking this aperitif. I have used Dolin Blanc vermouth here. Although slightly sweeter than dry vermouths, it has the advantage of being quite floral, without the strong spices and bittering agents that may compete with something as herbaceous and strong as basil. This also means the final vermouth pairs well with spirits like Pisco and tequila, leaving you open to further experimentation with your aperitifs. Try it in the Basil-infused Dolin Blanc Spritz (see page 152). Bon appétit!

25 large fresh basil leaves

700 or 750ml bottle of Dolin Blanc vermouth

1-quart (1-liter) wide-mouthed, sealable jar, sterilized (see page 24)

Fine-mesh strainer and muslin/ cheesecloth or coffee filter (see page 20)

Sealable presentation bottle(s), sterilized (see page 24)

Makes approximately 1½ pints (750ml)

Smack the basil leaves between your hands to release the essential oils. Place the leaves in the sterilized jar and pour in the vermouth. Seal the jar, upend a couple of times, and place somewhere cool and dark overnight. In the morning, fine-strain the liquid (see page 25) into a wide-mouthed pitcher, funnel into the sterilized presentation bottle(s), and seal. Store in the refrigerator and consume within 2 months.

Simply serve over ice with some sparkling water or add ¼oz (7ml) of your basil-infused vermouth to 3oz (90ml) vodka for a Martini with a refreshing twist.

VARIATION

Try replacing the basil with shiso if you would like to give the vermouth a slightly hotter twist.

PORCINI-INFUSED
Amontillado sherry

Sherry is, on average, 30–40 proof/15–20% ABV. This relatively low level of alcohol puts it in the danger zone for long infusions, as organic material can start to ferment and a few harmful bacteria can survive up to 34 proof/17% ABV. That said, quick infusions consumed within a short time (i.e. two weeks) can produce some wonderful results. Sherries have made a fantastic resurgence in the low-alcohol aperitif market because their flavor profile is so exciting. They also pair very well with food and other types of alcohol. From a crisp, dry, unaged fino or manzanilla to the relatively heavy, sweet cream and Pedro Ximénez varieties, they differ hugely in complexity. Here I used amontillado, which is an aged fino and fortified to around 36 proof/18% ABV. It has a nutty finish and anyone who has had the dish of mushrooms, sherry, and cream knows that these make a wonderful combination. Porcini mushrooms (*Botelus edulis*) hold their intensely nutty flavor very well when dried. When the dried mushrooms are blitzed into a powder they impart an incredible umami flavor to cocktails. Try this infusion in the Sherry and Aquafaba Aperitif (see page 158) or in Into The Woods (see page 170), where the powder is also used in a rich, savory seasoning for the rim of the glass.

3½oz (100g) dried porcini mushrooms
2 cups (500ml) amontillado sherry

Food blender or coffee grinder
1-quart (1-liter) wide-mouthed, sealable jar, sterilized (see page 24)
Fine-mesh strainer and muslin/cheesecloth or coffee filter (see page 20)
Sealable presentation bottle(s), sterilized (see page 24)

Makes approximately 1 pint (500ml)

Blitz the dried mushrooms into a very fine powder in the blender, then add this to the sterilized jar. Pour the sherry over the powder, ensuring that this remains submerged. Leave to infuse overnight. Fine-strain the infusion (see page 25) into a wide-mouthed pitcher, funnel into the sterilized presentation bottle(s), seal, and keep refrigerated. Consume within 2 weeks.

For a special occasion, try using a tablespoon of this infused sherry topped up with champagne!

Mushrooms are the best non-animal source of vitamin D and also contain many of the B vitamins.

Mushrooms are one of the few ingredients that have a more intense flavor when dried rather than fresh. Porcini mushrooms have a particularly strong flavor, so you only need to use a small amount. Play around with other mushrooms if you'd like more earthy notes.

Gorse RUM

Gorse (*Ulex europaeus*) can be found growing nearly everywhere and pretty much all year round. From coastal areas to heathland, town parks to urban wastelands, this acid-yellow and protein-rich jewel has extraordinary coconut and almond notes, making it a prize fit for rum. The price you pay for gathering gorse flowers is thorns in your fingers, as this extremely dense, spiny shrub doesn't offer up its prize lightly. As coconut and almonds go well together, there is no reason why you shouldn't also add some almond-tasting rowan (*Sorbus aucuparia*) buds and pineapple weed (*Matricaria discoidea*) flowers, which taste really pineapple-y, if you can find any. They make a valuable contribution to tiki-style drinks, or can be savored on their own with some ice and sparkling water. This particular infusion goes spectacularly well in the Gorse and Cherry Blossom Gimlet (see page 160).

gorse

2 cups (about 4 handfuls) fresh gorse flowers
Finely grated zest of 1 orange
2 tsp (10ml) raw honey
700 or 750ml bottle of white rum

1-quart (1-liter) wide-mouthed, sealable jar, sterilized (see page 24)
Fine-mesh strainer and muslin/ cheesecloth or coffee filter (see page 20)
Sealable presentation bottle(s), sterilized (see page 24)

Makes approximately 1½ pints (750ml)

Gently remove any wildlife or leaves from the gorse flowers and then put the flowers in the sterilized jar. Add the orange zest, honey, and rum. Seal the jar, upend a couple of times, and store overnight in a cool, dark place. Fine-strain the mixture (see page 25) into a wide-mouthed pitcher, then funnel into presentation bottle(s). Seal the bottle(s) and keep in a cool, dark place for 6 months.

To make the gorse-picking experience (and your drink) even better, pick your gorse blossoms in the morning on a warm day after the dew has lifted, but before the sun is at its hottest. This is when the blossoms will be packed with maximum flavor from their essential oils. (This applies to other flowers, such as roses and honeysuckle, too.)

Wild Homemade AQUAVIT

Our love affair with all things Scandinavian has extended to aquavit, their traditional spirit. Aquavit is a neutral spirit flavored with caraway and/or dill. However, in the same way that gin is flavored with a supporting cast of botanicals alongside the juniper, so too do commercial aquavits feature other ingredients, including fennel, citrus peel, cloves, juniper, star anise, ginger, and cardamom. This makes it an ideal spirit to make at home, using foraged and/or garden ingredients. There is no right or wrong recipe. You can dial up the bitter and bolder licorice notes of caraway or be more subtle using other ingredients. Tarragon leaves and fennel fronds can also lend a hand if it is too early in the season for fennel seeds and you are generous with them.

4 tsp of a selection of the following fruits/seeds: caraway fruits and/ or fennel seeds, wild carrot seeds, angelica seeds, sweet cicely seeds

2 cardamom pods, crushed (or 2 tsp hogweed seeds)

Small handful of dried herb bennet (*Geum urbanum*) roots, finely chopped (or 1 clove)

Grated zest of ½ lemon

Grated zest of ½ orange

1 tsp (5ml) honey

700 or 750ml bottle of vodka, preferably 100 proof/50% ABV

3 tarragon sprigs (optional)

3 long fennel fronds (optional)

1-quart (1-liter) wide-mouthed sealable jar, sterilized (see page 24)

Fine-mesh strainer and muslin/ cheesecloth or coffee filter (see page 20)

Sealable presentation bottle(s), sterilized (see page 24)

Makes approximately 1½ pints (750ml)

Toast all the spices (apart from the herb bennet) in a skillet/frying pan over a medium heat until you can smell their fragrance (about 2 minutes). Remove from the heat and drop the spices, along with the chopped herb bennet root, into the sterilized jar.

Add the citrus zests and honey. Pour the vodka into the jar, seal, and store in a cool, dark place for about 2 weeks. After 2 weeks, taste and see if you want to add any further spices. If using tarragon leaves and fennel fronds, smack them between your palms to release their essential oils and drop them into the infusion for a maximum of 2 days (otherwise they will make the aquavit taste vegetal). Fine-strain the infusion (see page 25) into a wide-mouthed pitcher and funnel into the sterilized presentation bottle(s). Store in the freezer.

Enjoy your aquavit straight from the freezer and use it to spice up a homemade Bloody Mary.

Caraway (*Carum carvi*) has one of the most aromatic flavors of all—it is mainly used for its licorice notes. Foraged alternatives include the seeds of wild fennel (*Foeniculum vulgare*), wild carrot (*Daucus carota*), common hogweed (*Heracleum sphondylium*), and wild angelica (*Angelica sylvestris*); the roots of herb bennet (*Geum urbanum*); and most parts of sweet cicely (*Myrrhis odorata*).

The small seeds of true anise (*Pimpinella anisum*) also have a licorice-like flavor. It does not grow wild in the U.K. or North America, but can be cultivated in frost-free areas. Star anise (*Illicium verum*) also has very potent licorice notes, but should be used sparingly. Licorice root (*Glycyrrhiza glabra*) provides a bittersweet alternative.

(For more on some of these useful plants, see *Chapter 2: Plants with Benefits*, pages 26–43.)

CHAPTER 4
DRINK OR MIX

However excited we may get about one aspect of a mocktail or cocktail, whether it's the acidity, the strength of the alcohol, or the bitterness of a herb, the clue is in the title—it's a cocktail of sensations. It all comes down to balance and experimentation, and there are many different methods and ingredients you can play with. Whether you wish to accentuate strong, floral, bitter, sour, or herbaceous flavors, you nearly always need an element of sweetness, if only a small, subtle measure, to balance everything out. The recipes in this chapter contain just enough sweetness, using the most healthy and delicious ingredients possible. I have favored using raw honey—usually two parts, or at least one and a half parts honey, to one part water—as a sweetener, but in the smallest possible quantities and substituted whole sweet fruit or sweet herbs where I can to get the balance right. Some of the recipes can be sipped as they are, but most need some ice and sparkling water at the very least. The idea is to play around with ingredients and flavors, depending on what's local, healthy, and delicious for you.

THE PARTS OF THE SUM

The recipes in this chapter can either be the star of the show or form a delicious part of the sum when you are creating an array of spectacular mocktails and cocktails.

CORDIALS/SYRUPS

Cordials and syrups are simply a high concentration of sweetener and water, which is used to extract maximum flavor from a plant material. In this book, I have avoided using refined sugar, but, as with a chef and salt in the world of food, so a bartender needs to have a sweetener to balance out very bitter or very acidic flavors. For all its evils, sugar—including natural sweeteners in the form of fructose in fruit, other plants, or honey—is a great extractor of flavor, as well as being an efficient preservative. You can reduce the amount of sweetener in your cordials by using sweet herbs, such as stevia or sweet cicely, or by combining sweet fruits with more tart or sour ones. Fruit is a good source of fiber, vitamins, and minerals, and is only used in small quantities in these recipes. Flavored syrups are wonderful because you can either drink them on their own as a soda, with ice and water, or include them in a mocktail/cocktail of your choice.

SODAS

Sodas are simply fruit or herbs in chilled still or soda water, which is then carbonated with CO_2 to extract their flavor and make the drink fizzy. You can do this using a soda maker, such as a SodaStream, and CO_2 cartridges (see page 21). The key to good carbonation is to have really chilled water, because carbon dioxide carbonates cold liquids much more effectively.

TONIC WATER

Tonic water is traditionally carbonated water that contains quinine and was originally created to ward off malaria. Nowadays we use tonic water for its distinctive bitter flavor—with a reduced level of quinine and lots more aromatics and bitter ingredients to make it more interesting. (For my recipe for homemade tonic water, see page 78.)

SHRUBS/VINEGARS

Derived from the Arab word *sharab*, which means "to drink," shrubs or "drinking vinegars" are simply a combination of vinegar, sweetener, and (usually) fruit. Besides being a great preservative, vinegar is also wonderful for extracting minerals. Shrubs can be made with every type of fresh fruit, vinegar, and sweetener, making them highly versatile drinks. They can be made using a cold maceration of sweetener and plant material over a few days to extract the plant's flavor and then combined with vinegar, or made instantly with a hot method by making a cordial (see left) and adding an equal part of vinegar. The combination of sweet and acid provides balance. A shrub can add complexity to a drink and you only need a tiny amount for its impact to be felt.

Shrubs may be added to sparkling water or fruit juice over ice, or used in very small amounts in a mocktail/cocktail to provide acid sweetness.

BITTERS

Bitters are everywhere in the plant kingdom. All plants contain catechins, tannins, terpenes, flavonoids, and alkaloids—and these are all bitter. But these compounds vary enormously in the intensity of bitterness found in different plants. Bitters are used in the drinks world to provide a seasoning in the same way that salt, pepper, herbs, and spices are used in cooking. They have a medicinal history, often being used in the past to stimulate appetite, aid digestion, and cure any number of ills. The sensation of bitter can excite and satisfy your taste buds in the same way that sweet can, which means you can gradually wean yourself off sugar and onto bitter. Just a dash of concentrated bitters can add a real complexity to your drinks. They are no more than bitter botanicals extracted in high-proof alcohol (or glycerin if you don't want to use alcohol) and made either with or without the addition of sweetener.

AMARI

Amaro (the singular form of amari) is just a general name for a bitter, herbal liqueur that is traditionally served after a meal to aid digestion (that is, a *digestif*), though it can also be used in a range of cocktails before and after dinner. The bitter and herbal complexity of amari works really well with other spicy elements in a drink. You can serve amari on their own over ice, with a mixer of your choice, or as part of a more complex cocktail.

As with most spirits—and certainly those that have a bitter component—amari started out as a cure for various maladies, from cholera to colic. Amari vary enormously in their flavor profile, from incredibly bitter to bitter-sweet. There are many commercial amari available, from the ubiquitous Jägermeister to mild Averna and incredibly bitter Fernet Branca.

It's entirely down to the available ingredients and your personal taste when it comes to deciding how bitter, citrusy, vegetal, or nutty you want to go. The process essentially involves macerating a neutral grain alcohol with whatever roots, herbs, and other botanicals you can get hold of in the wild, in your garden, at your local market, and/or online. A sweetener is then added. Some people age amari for years, while others believe that two weeks is plenty if you have used a high-proof alcohol.

The key to a good amaro is to use a high-proof alcohol (a minimum of 90–100 proof/45–50% ABV vodka, if you can find it), because it is very difficult to truly extract the bitterness you are aiming for without the aid of a high proof/ABV. As I am trying to reduce the use of sweeteners in this book, you don't want your amaro to be too bitter, as this will require counterbalancing that bitterness with a lot of sweetener. So it's a juggling act. As with bitters, it's down to playing and experimentation until you get a balance that suits your taste, but the key is to lay down a good base of bitterness on which the other flavors can play.

LIQUORI

The only difference between amari and liquori is that liquori can be made with fruit, such as lemons or cherries, and other solids. However, they are essentially made in the same way as amari: with a simple infusion method. The idea behind adding fruit here is to reduce the amount of additional sweetener that is required.

sweet cicely

flowering currant

Cherry Blossom
AND FLOWERING CURRANT CORDIAL

This is an exquisite cordial that requires gentle handling. You only need to add a tiny amount to a drink for maximum effect. To capture the delicate, almond-y scent and flavor of cherry blossom, steep it in hot, not boiling, water. A regular "boil" would burn the petals and leave you with an unpleasant vegetal liquid. This also applies to other delicate blossoms such as honeysuckle. Your patience will be amply rewarded in The Cherry Blossom (see page 104) and the Gorse and Cherry Blossom Gimlet (see page 160), or you can simply drink this cordial with ice and soda.

6 cups (about a small basket) cherry blossoms

15 heads of flowering currant (*Ribes sanguineum*) blossoms

1¼ cups (425g) local raw honey (as light-colored and unflavored as possible)

Large nonreactive saucepan
Fine-mesh strainer and cheesecloth/ muslin or coffee filter (see page 20)
Sealable heatproof presentation bottle(s), sterilized (see page 24)

Makes approximately 1 pint (500ml)

Remove any wildlife, stalks, and other debris from the cherry and flowering currant blossoms. Bring a saucepan of water to a boil, using just enough to cover the blossoms, and let cool to about 175°F (80°C). Submerge the blossoms in the water and let steep for 24 hours.

Fine-strain the liquid (see page 25) into a wide-mouthed pitcher, squeezing the blossoms to ensure all the flavorsome liquid is captured.

Clean the pan, pour in the strained liquid, and bring to a boil again. Allow the liquid to reduce by about a fifth to concentrate the flavor. Let cool slightly, then add the honey. When adding the honey, ensure you use a ratio of 1:1 honey to liquid (in volume, not weight, as honey is very heavy). Heat the liquid gently, stirring until the honey dissolves. Don't allow the honey to boil, or you will destroy the goodies in it.

Funnel your cordial into the sterilized presentation bottle(s) and let cool before storing in the refrigerator. Consume within 2 months.

KUMQUAT, THYME, CINNAMON, and *Honey Syrup*

This beautifully fragrant, citrusy, herbaceous, and warming syrup works with a variety of drinks, such as the Toasted Kumquat and Amaretto Sour (see page 164). You only need a very small amount of the syrup for it to make a delicious contribution to a mocktail or cocktail. I used raw honey to act as a sweetener, but also to help extract the flavor of the kumquats and thyme. To preserve the beneficial properties of the honey, I suggest you add it to the pan once the kumquats have been removed from the heat. As you are doing this, you can also add some citric acid to help preserve the syrup. However, if you are going to use the syrup within a couple of weeks, there is no need to add any citric acid, as long as you store it in the refrigerator between uses.

20 kumquats, halved lengthwise
1 cup (250ml) water
1 x 3-in (7.5-cm) cinnamon stick
2 cups (640g) raw runny honey
3 thyme sprigs
⅔ tsp citric acid (optional)

Nonreactive saucepan (with lid)
Wooden spoon
Fine-mesh strainer and muslin/cheesecloth or coffee filter (see page 20)
Sealable heatproof presentation bottle(s), sterilized (see page 24)

Makes approximately ½ pint (250ml)

Add the kumquats, water, and cinnamon stick to the saucepan and heat until just boiling. Lower the heat, cover the pan, and simmer for 5 minutes.

Remove from the heat and immediately add the honey and sprigs of thyme, stirring constantly to ensure the honey is fully dissolved. Allow the syrup to steep until cool (this will take at least 1 hour).

Reheat the syrup so that it is piping hot, but not boiling, add the citric acid (if using), and then fine-strain (see page 25) into a wide-mouthed pitcher. Funnel into the sterilized presentation bottle(s) and seal. Store in the refrigerator. If you have added citric acid, the syrup will last for up to 6 months. If not, consume within 2 weeks.

Thyme and LICORICE SYRUP

This can be used as a cough syrup, but is also an excellent source of tasty sweetness when combined with anise-y ingredients in a range of mocktails and cocktails.

3 tbsp fresh licorice (*Glycyrrhiza glabra*) root, chopped, or 1½ tbsp dried licorice root

2 cups (500ml) water

4 large thyme sprigs or 2 tbsp dried thyme

7oz (200g) raw honey

Nonreactive saucepan (with lid)

Fine-mesh strainer and cheesecloth/ muslin or coffee filter (see page 20)

Sealable heatproof presentation bottle(s), sterilized (see page 24)

Makes approximately 1 pint (500ml)

Add the fresh or dried licorice root to the water in the saucepan and bring to a gentle boil. Reduce the heat, cover the pan, and let simmer for 20 minutes. Remove the pan from the heat, add the fresh or dried thyme, and leave to infuse for a further 20 minutes.

Fine-strain the mix (see page 25) into a wide-mouthed pitcher, then return to a clean pan. Heat again until piping hot, but not boiling. Add the honey and stir continuously until this has dissolved, but do not allow the mix to boil.

As soon as the honey has dissolved completely, remove the pan from the heat. While it's still piping hot, funnel the syrup into the sterilized presentation bottle(s) and seal. Store in a dark, cool place and consume within 6 months.

Thyme

CITRUS BITTERS

As this book is all about maximizing flavor and maintaining balance in your cocktails, while dialing down the sweetness, the use of tiny drops of bitters to "season" drinks with sweet, bitter, and acid notes is very useful. While we consider bitters to be just that—bitter—many do, in fact, provide much more complex notes, with sweetness being one of them. Citrus combines acid and sugar, as well as the bitterness from the limonene in the zest. Using a variety of citrus fruits will naturally bring you an even wider range of flavors. You are also creating a wonderful aroma in your cocktails, your sense of smell being an important sense to trigger in an aperitif. In these bitters, the warm aromatic and bitter notes come from a mixture of foraged or store-bought ingredients, which are all available online.

angelica

1-quart (1-liter) wide-mouthed, sealable jar, sterilized (see page 24)

Fine-mesh strainer and muslin/ cheesecloth or coffee filter (see page 20)

4 x 5oz (150ml) or 10 x 2oz (60ml) dropper bottles, sterilized (see page 24)

Makes approximately 1 pint (500ml)

Although you are making a far greater quantity here than you will realistically consume yourself, homemade bitters make a wonderful gift and, besides, to work with even tinier quantities would be very tricky. For the amount of work involved, you may as well share the joy!

Finely chopped zest of the following unwaxed, organic citrus fruits (feel free to vary the combination): 4 grapefruits, 6 lemons, 10 limes, 6 oranges, 6 bergamot lemons

1 tsp dried angelica root

1 tbsp dried hogweed (*Heracleum sphondylium*) seeds (or 1 tbsp coriander seeds)

Large handful of herb bennet (*Geum urbanum*) roots, washed and finely chopped (or 2 allspice berries, crushed)

6 angelica seeds (or 6 cardamom pods)

1 tsp dried cut gentian root

1 tsp dried cut *Cinchona* bark

1 tsp freshly grated ginger

1 tsp dried field marigold (*Calendula arvensis*) leaves

4oz (125ml) dry Marsala wine or dry sherry

1¾ cups (450ml) high-proof vodka, 100 proof/50% ABV minimum (as high a proof as you can get)

Put all the ingredients in the sterilized jar. Seal and shake the jar, then store in a cool, dark place for 1 week, tasting daily in case you get a sufficiently strong taste sooner.

Fine-strain the bitters (see page 25) into a wide-mouthed pitcher and allow the contents to settle. If there is any sediment, repeat the process. Funnel the strained bitters into the sterilized bottles. Label the bottles (if you are liable to forget what is in them) and store them in a cool, dark place. Consume within 18 months.

You can use these Citrus Bitters in Roast Quince, Szechuan Pepper, Juniper, and Star Anise Mocktail (see page 138), Strawberry and Lemon Verbena Mocktail (see page 142), Fruity and Flowery Summer Mocktail (see page 149), Basil-infused Dolin Blanc Spritz (see page 152), and Into the Woods (see page 170).

FEATURED FORAGER: BECKY WYNN GRIFFITHS

Maker and purveyor of exquisite fruit liqueurs and the proprietor of Mother's Ruin Gin Palace—an old munitions warehouse on an industrial estate in east London—it was only a matter of time before my path crossed with that of Becky Wynn Griffiths. We have been stocking Becky's amazing libations at Midnight Apothecary for good reason. They are flipping delicious. From Gooseberry and Elderflower Vodka to Damson Gin and Rhubarb Vodka, this Mother really knows how to extract and develop flavor. The 12- to 18-month period of cold infusion is what creates the intense and well-rounded flavor of her delicious, award-winning liqueurs.

Raised on a farm in the Lyth Valley, in Cumbria, U.K., but currently living in Walthamstow, east London, for Becky the link between the land and food has never been broken. She has a community garden in London and an orchard in Cumbria, both dripping in damsons, and also finds plenty of rich pickings to be foraged near her London home. She generously invited me to one of her treasured foraging spots—an abandoned Victorian orchard on the outskirts of east London.

Up a winding footpath, in a busy urban area, were few signs of anything special: yellowy-green apples hidden among brambles with hops growing through them, if you looked closely. On closer inspection, there were barely detectable paths leading steeply through the undergrowth to an incredible sight: bright red jewels against a crisp fall/autumn sky, as a plateau of beautiful, gnarled apple trees of every variety stood barely hidden among the hawthorn, brambles, and long grass.

There were signs of human activity in the form of a few well-worn paths to some secret treasured trees. Becky told me that the pears had already been snaffled, but there was abundance everywhere. Even though a lack of pruning for many decades meant that some of the apples were now tiny and indistinguishable from crab apples, there were some good-sized specimens glinting red and green against the blue sky. With far-reaching views of high-rise apartments, it was a haunting but magical mélange of invasion and abandonment, glut and treasure. When so much of London has been reclaimed and gentrified, it makes discoveries like this all the more enchanting.

Becky's PEAR, QUINCE, AND APPLE WINDFALL BITTERS

Becky very kindly slipped a bottle of this elixir into one of our consignments of booze. It works particularly well with autumnal and winter libations that are heavy on whisky or brandy. These windfall bitters are really worth the effort. As Becky says, "You are aiming to build layers of flavor over about six weeks or so." You can also make a lovely crumble using the leftover flesh from the apples and quince. Try using these bitters in the Windfall Punch (see page 110) or the Quince Delight (see page 160).

pear

3 x 1-quart (1-liter) wide-mouthed, sealable jars, sterilized (see page 24)
Fine-mesh strainer and muslins/cheesecloths or coffee filters (see page 20)
Sealable presentation bottle(s), sterilized (see page 24)

Makes approximately 1½ pints (750ml)

Stage 1
700 or 750ml bottle of over-proof bourbon, 100 proof/50% ABV minimum (otherwise it will not extract the flavors properly)
Peel of 3 apples, coarsely chopped (ideally Bramley apples, if you can get them)
Peel of 2 large quince, coarsely chopped
Peel and roughly chopped flesh of 2 pears
Chopped zest of 1 lemon

Put all the ingredients in a sterilized jar, shake well, and leave somewhere cool and dark for 2 weeks. Shake occasionally.

Stage 2
1 cinnamon stick, cracked by hand
½ tsp allspice berries
½ tsp coriander seeds
6 cloves
Vanilla bean (pod), cut open and the seeds scraped out

Add the Stage 2 ingredients (including the vanilla seeds) to the jar, shake well, and leave as before, but this time for only 1 week.

Stage 3
4–5 *Quassia* bark chips
1 tsp dried burdock leaf

Add the Stage 3 ingredients to the jar, shake well, and leave for 1 week.

Stage 4
Fine-strain the liquid (see page 25) and set aside in a sterilized jar. Place the remaining solids in a pan, adding just enough water to cover, bring to a boil, then reduce the heat and simmer for 10 minutes.

Cool and place everything—the reduced solids and the liquid they were boiled in—in another sterilized jar. Leave for 1 week in a cool, dark place, shaking this new jar daily.

Stage 5
1½oz (45ml) Honey Syrup (see page 16)

Strain the liquid from the jar of solids and discard the solids. Combine the strained liquid with the liquid you retained at the start of Stage 4, then fine-strain (see page 25) the liquid again. Add the Honey Syrup. Shake well. Leave for 3 days, then strain again. Funnel the finished mixture into the sterilized presentation bottle(s) and knock up a very fine cocktail using several dashes of your spiced bitters.

Homemade
TONIC WATER SYRUP

I find that most tonic waters are too sweet and would far rather my taste buds and appetite were aroused by the sensation of bitterness. This tonic recipe is designed to provide just that, without using any refined sugar and with a burst of aromatics and citrus zest that won't overpower the beautiful botanicals in a well-crafted gin. This is a halfway house between a decoction (see page 95) and a cold maceration, and takes three days to complete. You want the essential oils and the flavor of the quinine in the tough cinchona bark to be fully extracted; hence the long, low boil of the "quinine tea." However, you also want to preserve the citrus and aromatic freshness of the citrus peel and lemongrass by not heating them—hence the cold maceration.

Instead of having your tonic already carbonated in soda water, this recipe provides the tonic syrup and then you just need to add sparkling water when you serve your drink. You can use either store-bought sparkling water or, alternatively, still water that you've carbonated yourself with carbon dioxide (CO_2) using a soda maker and CO_2 cartridges (see page 21). The finished tonic water is delicious as a mocktail in its own right or with any flavor combination you choose. Try it in the Basil-infused Dolin Blanc Spritz (see page 152).

Honey goes magnificently with gin, but I've chosen the lightest possible flavor and color

alexander flowerhead

here so that it doesn't clash with the many botanicals in the gin. Plus, you don't need to stick to gin; you could also use vodka, for example. I've also used a mix of foraged spices, but have provided store-bought alternatives in brackets too.

Caution: *Cinchona* bark is used to make homemade tonic because it contains quinine. However, it's important not to overdose on quinine and to strain your infusion thoroughly so it is free of quinine solids. This is why I don't suggest using powdered quinine, as it is more difficult to strain out the particles.

Nonreactive saucepan (with lid)

1-quart (1-liter) wide-mouthed, sealable jar, sterilized (see page 24)

Fine-mesh strainer and muslins/cheesecloths or coffee filters (see page 20)

Wooden spoon

Sealable presentation bottle(s), sterilized (see page 24)

GIN AND HOMEMADE TONIC

To make a refreshing gin and tonic, combine 1½oz (45ml) gin, ¾oz (22ml) Homemade Tonic Water Syrup, and 3oz (90ml) sparkling water over ice cubes in a large red wine glass or highball glass. Garnish with a wedge of lime and something herbaceous!

For the tonic syrup:

4 cups (1 liter) water

¼ cup (30g) chopped *Cinchona* bark (not powdered)

Peeled zest of 3 unwaxed, organic lemons

Peeled zest of 3 unwaxed, organic limes

Peeled zest of 1 unwaxed, organic orange

Peeled zest of 1 unwaxed, organic grapefruit

4 lemongrass stalks, trimmed of their outer layer, stalks bashed, and chopped into ¼-in (5-mm) pieces

5 fresh birch (*Betula pubescens*) leaves (or 2 dried kefir lime leaves)

20 hogweed (*Heracleum sphondylium*) seeds (or 6 green cardamom pods)

20 alexander (*Smyrnium olusatrum*) seeds, dried and toasted (or 9 allspice berries)

Small handful (about 6 pieces) of fine herb bennet (*Geum urbanum*) roots, about 3in (7.5cm) long, finely chopped (or 3 cloves)

1 star anise

1 tbsp culinary-grade lavender buds

¼ cup (35g) citric acid

¼ tsp kosher seasalt

For the honey syrup:

2 cups (640g) light, raw, runny honey

1½ cups (350ml) water

Makes approximately 1 quart (1 liter)—enough for 70 cocktails!

To make the tonic syrup, pour the water into the saucepan, add the chopped cinchona bark, and bring to a boil. As soon as the liquid reaches boiling point, cover and simmer for 20 minutes. Let cool, then fine-strain the liquid (see page 25), using at least two coffee filters or several layers of cheesecloth/muslin, into a wide-mouthed pitcher—you really don't want solid quinine particles in your tonic syrup.

Fill the sterilized jar with all the other ingredients. Pour the cold "quinine tea" over the mix in the jar, seal, shake, and store somewhere dark and dry for 3 days, shaking once each day.

To make the honey syrup, warm the honey with the water in a pan over a medium heat, stirring until the honey has dissolved and the water is just below boiling point. Let cool and refrigerate until needed.

Fine-strain the tonic syrup again (see page 25) through several layers of muslin/cheesecloth or coffee filters into a wide bowl. Pour the honey syrup into the bowl and whisk thoroughly to combine. Funnel the finished tonic syrup into the sterilized presentation bottle(s) and then store in the refrigerator for the duration of the summer.

To enjoy refreshing homemade tonic water, simply mix ¾oz (22ml) of the tonic syrup with 3oz (90ml) sparkling water over ice, per serve.

lavender

Wild Sour Cherry and
FLOWERING CURRANT SODA

If you have found some gorgeous wild or cultivated sour cherries (*Prunus cerasus*), this is a great way to extract their flavor instantly in a healthy carbonated mixer that contains no added sugar. The process simply involves pouring liquid into a sealed vessel, adding carbon dioxide, and shaking to combine the gas and liquid. If you do this with soda water, you get a club soda; if you add quinine and citrus, you have tonic water; and if you add syrup, you'll get an instant mocktail. You can buy quite sophisticated home units for adding carbonation, but investing in a good-quality professional cream whipper will allow you to use both CO_2 cartridges for carbonation and N_2O (nitrous oxide) cartridges for rapid infusions and foams. The trick with carbonation is to use really cold liquid—in this case, the soda water and cherry juice—because CO_2 carbonates liquids more thoroughly when they are cold. You could just use the juice of the cherries, but I like to give everything a head start with some soda water. You can use this soda in The Cherry Blossom (see page 104).

12 ripe sour cherries, stoned (pitted)

5 heads of flowering currant (*Ribes sanguineum*) blossoms

⅓ cup (100ml) soda water, chilled

Muddler
Mixing glass
Soda maker and CO_2 cartridge

Makes enough for 1 drink

Muddle (see page 24) the stoned (pitted) cherries thoroughly in the mixing glass, to extract as much juice as possible. Put in the freezer to cool for 30 minutes, then funnel the cold liquid into the soda maker. Add the flowering currant blossoms and chilled soda water, then charge the canister with one CO_2 cartridge, following the manufacturer's instructions. Shake the charger for 20 seconds and expel the gas. You now have a beautiful instant soda.

Sour cherries are bursting with vitamin C and antioxidants—lots more than their sweet cousins (*Prunus avium*). You can use the method described here for any soft fruit you wish to create some really delicious combinations.

VARIATION

You can add all manner of herbs and fruit to some chilled still water or put the water in a soda maker or professional cream whipper, and charge it with CO_2 to produce a tasty fizzy mixer. For example, try two handfuls of fresh pea shoots for a really refreshing mixer. Smack the shoots gently between your palms to release the oils before adding them to the soda maker or cream whipper. Even if you don't charge the water with CO_2 to make it fizzy, you've still got a delightfully subtle flavored water if you allow the herb to infuse in the water for at least 1 hour.

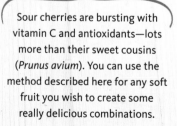

MAGNOLIA FLOWER
Vinegar

Magnolia flowers not only fill urban streets with an exotic display of botanical grandeur, but they taste incredible too. If you nibble on them raw, you will get a sense of their fragrant spiciness—they taste almost like meaty rose petals. Pickling them in vinegar brings out their ginger flavor. These are all very useful notes for your cocktail cabinet. You can use this method to make wild violet (*Viola odorata*) vinegar too. Of course, if you also add sugar and salt, then you will have a proper pickling liquid; however, here I just wanted the vinegar with none of the sweetness. It is best to look for younger blossoms and to pick them from a variety of trees so you don't strip any individual tree of blossom. You can use a tiny amount of this flower vinegar in The Cherry Blossom (see page 104).

1lb 2oz (500g) magnolia petals

2 cups (500ml) rice wine vinegar or champagne vinegar

1-pint (500-ml) sealable glass jar, sterilized (see page 24)

Makes approximately 1 pint (500ml)

Gently cram as many magnolia petals as you can into the sterilized jar before pouring in the vinegar—ensure the petals are completely immersed. Seal the jar and keep in a cool, dark place for at least 2 weeks. Strain your vinegar, as and when you need to use it. The petals will last in the jar for at least 6 months.

SPRING TONIC VINEGAR

This vinegar is a pleasure to collect, make, and drink, and is bursting with the joys of spring. There is no need to be too prescriptive. Nature throws us nutrient-dense, mineral-rich, and anti-inflammatory plants at this time of year to detoxify and revitalize our liver, kidneys, and blood. As long as you correctly identify what you've picked, you can't go too far wrong. Cleavers, as well as nettle, chickweed, dandelion, violet, and alexander leaves are perfect. You can also add violet, mahonia, and primrose flowers if you see any. Apple cider vinegar is particularly beneficial for your health, but if you want a smoother drink, use champagne or white wine vinegar instead. About 4 handfuls of finely chopped herbs in a 1-quart (1-liter) jar of vinegar is fine. Infuse for 2 weeks, strain (as above), and use in a tonic.

Magnolia and
CHERRY BLOSSOM SHRUB

Magnolia and cherry blossom trees flower at the same time in spring, so it seems sensible to combine the gingery notes of magnolia flowers with the almond-y taste of cherry blossoms. This recipe is essentially a combination of three other recipes in the book to create a sweet, salty, acidy shrub that can be drunk with sparkling water over ice. Here, I used the Magnolia Flower Vinegar (see page 81), the Cherry Blossom and Flowering Currant Cordial (see page 70), and some of the salty vinegar (often called Ume plum vinegar if store-bought) left over from making a batch of Sakura Tea (see page 103). If you haven't made any Sakura Tea, then simply steep some magnolia flowers in the Ume plum vinegar first, as this will give you the saltiness you require.

magnolia

5oz (150ml) Magnolia Flower Vinegar (see page 81)

7oz (200ml) Cherry Blossom and Flowering Currant Cordial (see page 70)

1½oz (45ml) Ume plum vinegar or salty vinegar from making some Sakura Tea (see page 103)

Fine-mesh strainer and muslin/cheesecloth or coffee filter (see page 20)

Nonreactive saucepan

Wooden spoon

1-quart (1-liter) wide-mouthed, sealable jar, sterilized (see page 24)

Sealable heatproof presentation bottle(s), sterilized (see page 24)

Makes approximately 1 pint (500ml)

If you haven't already fine-strained your magnolia petals (see page 25) when making a batch of Magnolia Flower Vinegar, do so now. Add the strained Magnolia Flower Vinegar, Cherry Blossom and Flowering Currant Cordial, and Ume plum vinegar/salty vinegar to the saucepan and heat gently, stirring to combine the cordial and vinegars thoroughly. Just before the liquid reaches boiling point, remove the pan from the heat. Pour the shrub, while it is still piping hot, into a wide-mouthed pitcher, then funnel into the sterilized presentation bottle(s) and seal. Store in a cool, dark place for 6 months.

To mix a delicious drink, simply combine ½–1oz (15–30ml) of the shrub with 8oz (240ml) sparkling water in an ice-filled highball glass.

cherry blossom

STRAWBERRY, CLOVER, *and* *Meadowsweet Shrub*

The sweetness of strawberries and red clover (*Trifolium pratense*) combined with the almond-y, honey flavor of meadowsweet (*Filipendula ulmaria*) flowers and the aromatics of meadowsweet seeds make for a delicious shrub. Strawberries are well known for their vitamin C content and high antioxidant levels. The unfiltered apple cider vinegar is packed with potassium and live enzymes, and helps to promote youthful skin, regulate calcium metabolism, lower blood pressure and cholesterol, aid digestion, and reduce chronic fatigue. It can also aid weight control. Not bad results from one ingredient! Letting the shrub ferment gently over a few days means it can also improve your digestion and help colonize your gut with healthy bacteria. Try this shrub in the Fruity and Flowery Summer Mocktail (see page 149).

4 heads of meadowsweet blossoms, fully opened

2 cups (400g) chopped organic strawberries

½ cup (about 15–20) red clover flowers

2 tsp meadowsweet seeds, if you have any from last year (optional)

1 cup (320g) raw, runny honey

1 cup (250ml) white balsamic vinegar

1 cup (250ml) organic, raw, unfiltered apple cider vinegar

1-quart (1-liter) wide-mouthed, sealable jar, with a nonreactive lid, sterilized (see page 24)

Wooden spoon or muddler

Fine-mesh strainer and muslin/ cheesecloth or coffee filter (see page 20)

Sealable presentation bottle(s), with nonreactive lid(s), sterilized (see page 24)

Makes approximately 1 pint (500ml)

Strip the meadowsweet blossoms of stems and stalks, and set them aside in order to give the wildlife plenty of time to disperse.

Put the strawberries in the sterilized jar. Add the clover and meadowsweet flowers, and meadowsweet seeds (if using). Using the end of the wooden spoon or muddler, lightly crush the fruit, blossoms, and seeds.

Add the honey and vinegars, and stir thoroughly to combine. It is important that you cover the jar with a glass or plastic (i.e. nonreactive) lid. Alternatively, if you are using a canning jar that has a metal lid, put a piece of parchment or waxed paper between the vinegar and the lid, to prevent it from corroding. Put the sealed jar in the refrigerator to infuse for 1 week, shaking gently every day.

Fine-strain the shrub (see page 25) into a wide-mouthed pitcher and funnel into the sterilized presentation bottle(s). Store in the refrigerator and consume within 6 months.

To create a delicious drink, simply mix ½–1oz (15–30ml) of the shrub with 8oz (240ml) sparkling water in an ice-filled highball glass.

Coumarin, the slightly vanilla-flavored phytochemical found in red clover, meadowsweet, sweet woodruff (*Galium odoratum*), and cleavers (*Galium aparine*), has antifungal and antitumor properties. It also thins the blood, especially if it is dried in damp conditions. However, you should only consume it in moderation and avoid it altogether if you are taking anticoagulants.

Sage~infused HAZELNUT OIL

Providing your taste buds and tongue with mouth-feel and not just flavor is essential, to replace the role that refined sugar plays in a cocktail. However, a drink will taste too "thin" without the viscosity of sugar and leave you feeling dissatisfied. As we now know that sugar is far more of an enemy than fat, here's an infused oil to the rescue.

There are two ways to use oil in a cocktail. The first is to float a few drops on the surface of the finished cocktail, which imparts a smooth texture, visual interest, and prominent flavors in your first sip. The second is to combine oil with an egg white and shake the cocktail really hard. The proteins in the egg white emulsify the alcohol and oil, to produce a rich, creamy cocktail. The oil is acting in pretty much the same way as an egg yolk in a Flip, though the resulting cocktail won't be quite as thick and viscous. You have about 15 minutes to down the cocktail before the oil separates. I'd say that's plenty of time.

You can use any oil you like. Olive oil imparts floral, grassy, peppery notes, but you may prefer to use locally grown oils. Here I wanted nuttiness but, more importantly, I wanted the oil to carry the flavor of sage (*Salvia officinalis*) so that I could use it in Into the Woods (see page 170). You can try any combination of fresh herbs (woody or soft), spices, citrus, and nuts in the infused oil. You can even try dried mushrooms (but not fresh ones).

2 cups (500ml) hazelnut oil
10 sage leaves

Small saucepan
Fine-mesh strainer and muslin/cheesecloth or coffee filter (see page 20)
Glass bottle(s) with tight-fitting cap(s) or cork(s), sterilized (see page 24)

Makes approximately 1 pint (500ml)

Warm the oil and sage in a small saucepan over a medium heat for about 5 minutes, until the oil is bubbling lightly. Remove from the heat and let the oil cool completely. Fine-strain the oil (see page 25) into a wide-mouthed pitcher, then funnel into the sterilized bottle(s). Seal and label the bottle(s) with the contents and "use-by" date (if you are liable to forget what they contain). This should be no longer than a month. Store in the refrigerator between uses.

It is important to refrigerate and consume the sage oil within a month, but bring it up to room temperature before using.

Citrus AMARO

To effectively extract maximum flavor from tough and bitter ingredients, such as bark and roots, you either need to use them to make a strong decoction (i.e. a tea) and then add this to a base alcohol later, or you have to tincture them in high-proof alcohol. When creating the ideal amaro, the challenge lies in macerating a wide range of plant material, some of which will be fresh and delicate, some dry and bitter, and all requiring slightly different infusion times. The idea with this recipe is to complete the entire infusion using two simple processes without a separate tincturing of the bitter roots and aromatic spices. I've found it's best not to over-do the length of time you macerate an ingredient (because otherwise it can become vegetal, dull, bitter, and/or overpowering). To avoid this, you need to use the highest proof alcohol you can get hold of and the shortest possible infusion time. We are effectively making a tincture of the whole recipe by using alcohol that is as close to 130–140 proof/65–70% ABV (the ideal level for extracting most essential oils) as possible, but only macerating it for a maximum of three weeks before straining it and adding a sweetener.

In the U.K., you can usually only buy vodka of about 80–100 proof/40–50% ABV, but there is now one available that is 176 proof/88% ABV, so this is what I've used here. However, it will need diluting with ice at the very least at the point of drinking!

If you can't find a strong vodka (that is, over 100 proof/50% ABV), tincture the roots and aromatic spices separately (see pages 56–57 for guidance on tincturing) and then add these in

nettle

small quantities (using a maximum of about 1–3 tsp/5–15ml of each) to the base alcohol—use a pipette to do this, so you don't overpower the other ingredients.

The first flavors to be released into the base alcohol are often the most delicate and bright, but they are also volatile. It seems a shame to dull these by using overpowering tannic and other flavors from over-done tinctures, hence the shortest tincture in the strongest possible booze.

You don't need to use all the ingredients listed overleaf. Just play around with what you have available. This recipe is citrusy and warmly aromatic, with the base of tangy bitterness coming from the gentian.

6 dried nettle (*Urtica dioica*) leaves

3 tsp (about 3 sprigs' worth) rosemary leaves

2 fresh ground ivy (*Glechoma hederacea*) sprigs or 1 dried sprig (or 6 mint leaves)

A handful (about 15) of fine herb bennet (*Geum urbanum*) roots, each about 6in (15cm) long and 1/16 in (2mm) wide, finely chopped

½ tsp hogweed (*Heracleum sphondylium*) seeds (or 2 cloves and 1 allspice berry)

½ tsp dried burdock root or 1 tbsp green hops (optional)

½ tsp gentian root

1 tsp fennel seeds

1 tsp angelica seeds

1 tsp angelica root, dried and chopped

1 star anise

Dried peel of 1 unwaxed, organic orange

Dried peel of 1 unwaxed, organic lemon

Dried peel of 1 unwaxed, organic grapefruit

700 or 750ml bottle of high-proof vodka (such as Balkan 176 vodka)

For the honey syrup:
2 cups (640g) raw, runny honey
1 cup (250ml) water

Pestle and mortar

1-quart (1-liter) wide-mouthed, sealable jar, sterilized (see page 24)

Fine-mesh strainer and muslins/ cheesecloths or coffee filters (see page 20)

Sealable presentation bottle(s), sterilized (see page 24)

Make about 1 quart (1 liter)

Finely chop all the herbs and roughly grind the spices to expose as much surface area as possible to the alcohol. Add the prepared herbs, spices, and citrus peels to the sterilized jar and pour in the vodka. Seal the jar, shake, and store in a cool, dark place for 3 weeks, shaking several times a week. If you notice that alcohol has evaporated or any of the plant material is not fully immersed, then top up the jar with more high-proof alcohol. Leave for 3 weeks, then fine-strain the mix (see page 25) through several layers of muslin/cheesecloth or coffee filters into a wide-mouthed pitcher.

To make the honey syrup, slowly heat the honey and water in a saucepan until the honey dissolves. Let cool and add the syrup to the strained amaro. Stir to combine and then funnel into the sterilized presentation bottle(s). Seal and shake the bottle(s), then wait 1 week to let the flavors blend before using. Lasts indefinitely.

mint

burdock root

Cherry and Cacao LIQUORE

As this recipe involves cherries and chocolate, I used grappa—a grape brandy made from the skins, pulp, and seeds of grapes (from the only English grappa producer in the U.K.). At about 90 proof/45% ABV, this grappa is not within the ideal 130–140 proof/65–70% ABV range for maximum infusion, so I used half grappa and half high-proof vodka. This liquore is not as bitter as the Citrus Amaro (see page 87), so I used grape molasses to sweeten it, which are not a particularly sweet type of molasses—they have a tartness. You can use something sweeter instead, such as date molasses or honey. Try this liquore in the Liquore Digestif (see page 159).

Pestle and mortar

1-quart (1-liter) wide-mouthed, sealable jar, sterilized (see page 24)

Fine-mesh strainer and muslins/cheesecloths or coffee filters (see page 20)

Sealable presentation bottle(s), sterilized (see page 24)

Makes approximately 1 quart (1 liter)

Figs

40 fresh cherries, stones (pips) in, but pierced to release their juices, or 20 dried cherries

2 figs, chopped into 8 segments

2 dates, stoned (pitted) and chopped

10 yellow raisins

2 tsp cacao nibs

5 almond shell husks

2 tsp wild cherry bark

1 x 6-in (15-cm) long fresh dandelion (*Taraxacum officinale*) root, finely chopped

3 x 6-in (15-cm) sweet woodruff (*Galium odoratum*) sprigs, dried

¼ cup (30g) chopped *Cinchona* bark (not powdered)

5 coffee beans

3 black peppercorns

½ cinnamon stick

12oz (350ml) high-proof vodka, 176 proof/88% ABV minimum (such as Balkan 176 vodka)

12oz (350ml) grappa, 86 proof/43% ABV minimum (such as Dappa from Devon Distillery)

10oz (300ml) grape molasses or 7oz (200ml) date molasses (or 10oz/300ml Honey Syrup, see page 16)

Roughly chop all the fruit and herb ingredients, and grind the spice ingredients, to expose as much surface area to the alcohol as possible, without turning anything into a paste or powder (because these will be difficult to strain). Put all the prepared ingredients in the sterilized jar.

Add the vodka and grappa to the jar, then seal, shake, and put somewhere cool, dark, and dry for 3 weeks. If you notice any alcohol has evaporated or any plant material is not fully immersed, top up with more high-proof alcohol.

Leave for 3 weeks, then fine-strain the mix (see page 25) through several layers of muslin/cheesecloth or coffee filters into a wide-mouthed pitcher. Let cool and add your chosen sweetener to the strained liquore. Stir to combine thoroughly and funnel into the sterilized presentation bottle(s). Seal and shake the bottle(s), then wait 1 week to let the flavors blend before using. Lasts indefinitely.

CHAPTER 5
TEA-BASED DRINKS

Tea has been combined with spirits on a large scale for hundreds of years in the form of punch. Without getting too hung up on whether alcohol or water is the best carrier of flavor and nutrients, it is obvious—when looking at the vast array of flavors along a tea aisle in a good food store—that tea is certainly a popular option. The advantage of using tea is apparent to non-drinkers and also those who would like the option of adding alcohol later if desired.

Tea-based cocktails are also getting more popular because they are low in sugar, relatively cheap, and can provide a complex cocktail for a large group of people with relatively little effort. Whether you are going down the traditional route of hot infusion or getting into cold-brew tea, there is a myriad combination of flavors to play with in your cocktail cuppa.

THE POWER OF TEA

How complicated the world gets. A few years ago I would have said that you could use a cold, alcohol-based infusion to extract taste and nutrients from a plant or go for a hot, water-based tea to do the same thing. But then along came cold-brew teas and coffees—and that put paid to that!

COLD-BREW TEAS

Cold or iced teas are growing in popularity. Cold water extracts a different chemical balance than hot water. Put simply, the cold-brew process reduces the catechins and caffeine, which dials out a lot of the bitterness. Herbs that lend themselves to this method include lemon balm, marjoram, and pineapple sage. The method then couldn't be simpler—it just takes time.

To make a cold-brew tea, add about 4 teaspoons of dried or a scant 3 tablespoons of fresh material (about one-and-a-half times the amount you would normally use in tea) to distilled water in a 1-quart (1-liter), sealable, sterilized (see page 24) jar or special brewpot, put it in the refrigerator, and wait for 4–10 hours (the length of time will depend on the ingredients you've used). Then simply strain and serve the cold tea in your teacup or glass. I hope you feel compelled to play around with this method to see how it compares with your regular cuppa. You can also use the strained tea in mocktails or cocktails of your choice.

HERBS SUITABLE FOR MAKING COLD-BREW TEAS

Anise (*Pimpinella anisum*)

Catnip (*Nepeta cataria*)

Honeysuckle (*Lonicera*)

Hyssop (*Hyssopus officinalis*)

Lemon balm (*Melissa officinalis*)

Lemon verbena (*Aloysia citrodora*)

Marjoram (*Origanum majorana*)

Orange (*Citrus sinensis*) blossom

Pineapple sage (*Salvia elegans*)

Rose (*Rosa*) petals

Caution: The dried herbs, flowers, or fruit used in the cold-brew method should have a quick rinse with boiling water before you get going, as they may harbor bacteria, and even fresh herbs can benefit from a rinse with some boiling water first to wake them up.

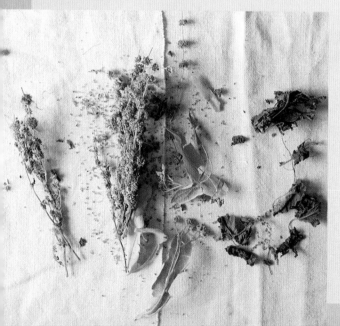

dried Tea ingredients

HOT-BREW TEAS

It's worth clearing up some of the terms used around making hot tea. Technically, the only true tea is made from a plant called *Camellia sinensis* and it's the method of processing, rather than the variety of tea, that determines whether this ends up as black, oolong, green, white, or pu-erh tea. True teas bring tannins (like wine) and a lovely astringent dryness to a cocktail, as well as lots of antioxidants. They add a subtle delicacy and aromatics. As a result, you can use "true teas" as you would a spice as an element in an infusion or cocktail.

Tisanes What is often referred to as an "herbal tea" is actually an infusion or decoction made from any plant other than *Camellia sinensis*. People often refer to herbal teas, which is what we are making in this chapter, as "tisanes."

Brewing times and proportions for tisanes vary widely. The time can be as short as 2 minutes or as long as 15 minutes—or even overnight if you are extracting flavor from a delicate flower such as cherry blossom—and the tea may require as little as a pinch of plant material per cup of water or as much as several tablespoons per cup. As a rule of thumb, I would suggest using one heaped teaspoon of dried herb per cup of water or three heaped teaspoons of fresh herb per cup of water.

To make a tisane, you simply bring the water to a boil and pour it over the plant matter. Leave to steep for 5 minutes, taste, and then continue to steep until you can detect a strong flavor of the ingredient you want. If you are steeping something very delicate, such as a flower petal, make sure the water is off a boil, or you will "burn" the flavor and the tea will taste vegetal.

You can make a tisane from multiple parts of the same plant or stick to a single type, such as a herb tisane from lemon verbena or mint, a flower tisane from roses or hibiscus, a bark tisane from cinnamon or black cherry bark, a root tisane from ginger or echinacea, a fruit or berry tisane from any number of fruits, and seed or spice tisanes from as wide a list as your imagination will go. Basically, all these categories are just the starting point to fire up your imagination. The combination of garden, foraged, or market ingredients is endless. Incidentally, a kombucha is often classified as a tisane, but it is technically a Symbiotic Colony of Yeast and Bacteria (or SCOBY)—see pages 120 and 122 for more information on kombucha.

rose

Decoctions These release more essential oils and flavor from the plant matter than tisanes, and are often used for those parts of a plant that have tough surfaces or smaller surface areas. The process involves boiling down the liquid containing the plant matter for between 10 minutes and 1 hour, and then steeping for several hours to form a concentrate that you later dilute. This method is sometimes used for making bitters and amari (see page 69), as well as for other medicinal applications. Bark and root tisanes are generally prepared as decoctions, as are some tough berries. The exception to this rule would be certain roots, such as ginger, where a tisane would be preferable due to the delicate essential oils that would be lost during the process of decoction.

The recipes in this chapter are divided into *Tisane Tipples* (see pages 96–107) that use herbs and other plants and *"True Tea" Tipples* (see pages 108–117), which use real tea to create a host of delicious drinks.

TISANE TIPPLES

As a tisane is simply a quantity of plant material that has been steeped in hot water, there are countless combinations of flavor, scent, and medicinal elements that you can play around with. I have suggested a few in this section, but you can adapt these according to what's growing near you or is in season at your local market.

All these teas can be drunk on their own, sweetened with a teaspoon of honey and served hot, and either with or without alcohol. Alternatively, they can be allowed to cool and served over ice with a teaspoon of honey as a mocktail or combined with your chosen alcohol, perhaps gin or vodka, and a splash of citrus and honey, then topped up with tonic or soda water—and also with bitters, if desired—as a long cocktail. As you are using citrus and honey here, you need to shake these drinks over ice in a cocktail shaker to blend all the ingredients, before straining into your cocktail glass or cup.

For hot drinks, you only need a single measure of alcohol (1oz/30ml), or the alcohol becomes overpowering. For cold drinks, you can use up to a double measure (2oz/60ml).

PINEAPPLE SAGE
and Scented Geranium Tea

The strong sweet aroma of pineapple sage (*Salvia elegans*) is tangy and calming. The aromatic lemony notes of scented geranium (*Pelargonium*) that I use here provide an additional complementary layer of flavor. This is a simple steeped tea that is delicious either hot or cold. Try it cold in a cocktail as part of The Bonfire of the Vani-Teas (see page 105).

7oz (200ml) boiling water
15 pineapple sage leaves
4 scented geranium leaves

Heatproof measuring pitcher, teapot (optional), teaspoon, tea strainer, serving cup(s)

**Makes 1 cup
(approximately ⅓ pint/200ml)**

Pour 7oz (200ml) of boiling water per serve over the sage and geranium leaves in either the pitcher or teapot (depending on the quantity you are making). Steep for 20 minutes. Let cool and then strain into your serving cup(s).

Pineapple sage is busting with anti-inflammatory, antioxidant, and antimicrobial properties. It is a source of vitamins A and K. It can relieve symptoms as varied as hot flashes/flushes experienced during the menopause, anxiety, and depression, as well as bacterial infections like sore throats. If that's not enough, it is also good for indigestion and gas. The only word of warning is to avoid pineapple sage if you are breastfeeding or pregnant because it contains thujone, which is a uterine stimulant.

BLACKCURRANT SAGE, WINTER SAVORY, and Lemon Verbena Tea

blackcurrant leaf

Blackcurrant sage (*Salvia microphylla*) produces a profusion of gorgeous scarlet flowers from mid-summer to mid-winter, which makes it a great plant for providing a garnish. But it is the amazing leaves—which taste so strongly of blackcurrant candies/sweets (maybe crossed with melon!)—that set it apart as a fantastic addition to a cocktail garden. The plant originates from South America and the leaves can be used fresh or dried, alongside the flowers, in a famous tea called *mirot de montes*, or "myrtle of the mountains," to treat fever. Here I've steeped it with some winter savory (*Satureja montana*), which can be used like thyme, but I think gives notes of pine, thyme, and pepper in one plant. The lemon verbena (*Aloysia citrodora*) offers up an exquisite lemony sweetness, but is one of those plants to use sparingly as it is very strong.

7oz (200ml) boiling water

3 tsp fresh or 1 tsp dried blackcurrant sage or small handful of fresh blackcurrant (*Ribes nigrum*) leaves

4 lemon verbena leaves

2-in (5-cm) winter savory sprig

Heatproof measuring pitcher, teapot (optional), teaspoon, tea strainer, serving cup(s)

Makes 1 cup (approximately ⅓ pint/200ml)

Pour 7oz (200ml) of boiling water per serve over the blackcurrant sage or blackcurrant leaves, lemon verbena leaves, and winter savory in either the pitcher or teapot (depending on the quantity you are making). Steep for 20 minutes. Let cool and then strain into your serving cup(s).

In Jamaica and other parts of the Caribbean, lemongrass is called "fever grass." It is made into a tea to combat fever and other cold/flu symptoms. Its relaxant properties are used to relieve stress and headaches. Lemongrass is high in manganese, folate (a B vitamin), vitamins B1, B5, and B6, potassium, iron, zinc, and even calcium. Lemongrass oil has effective anti-inflammatory and antibacterial properties, and is also used to treat diarrhea and to repel mosquitoes. A Malaysian adage says that you might discover treasure beneath a lemongrass plant if you find a lemongrass blossom, because they bloom so rarely!

To store fresh lemongrass, simply cut the leaves into 1½-in (3-cm) pieces and keep in a sealed container in the refrigerator or freezer.

Lemongrass TEA

This delicious drink can be served either with or without alcohol, but the shine-out star is the lemongrass (*Cymbopogon citratus*). I was lucky enough to be given some freshly picked leaves by Jekka McVicar (see *Featured Forager*, on page 35). The scent and flavor of this aromatic leaf (as opposed to the stalk) when fresh are bright and sublime. It is a combination of citrus, floral, grass, and ginger. It is milder and sweeter than lemon, and I find that if you combine it with some sweet and cooling cucumber, you don't need to add any additional sweetener to a mocktail or cocktail. Dried lemongrass stalks also make a delicious tea, but this will be less complex and more woods-y in flavor. I like to combine the dried stalks with a slice of ginger to give them added complexity. If you're using stalks, cut off the root end and remove any of the dry outer leaves. You will need to gently bruise the base of the stalks with a rolling pin to release the oil and flavor.

1-quart (1-liter) nonreactive, sealable container, sterilized (see page 24) or special brewpot, rolling pin (if using a lemongrass stalk), teaspoon, tea strainer, serving cup(s)

50 pieces of fresh lemongrass leaf (1½in/4cm long) or 2 chopped lemongrass stalks

2 slices peeled ginger, ¼in (6mm) thick (optional)

1 tsp (5ml) honey (optional)

1 tsp (5ml) freshly squeezed lime juice (optional)

1 quart (1 liter) distilled water

Makes approximately 1 quart (1 liter)

Cold-brew method:

Place the lemongrass leaves or stalks, plus the ginger, honey, and lime juice (if using), in the nonreactive, sterilized container and add the distilled water. (If you are using dried lemongrass, quickly rinse it in boiling water first, to remove any harmful bacteria and to wake it up.) Put the tea in the refrigerator for at least 6 hours (or overnight). Simply strain and serve as desired.

Heatproof measuring pitcher, teapot (optional), rolling pin (if using a lemongrass stalk), teaspoon, tea strainer, serving cup(s)

25–30 pieces of fresh lemongrass leaf (1½in/4cm long) or 1 chopped lemongrass stalk

7oz (200ml) boiling water

1 slice peeled ginger, ¼in (6mm) thick (optional)

1 tsp (5ml) honey (optional)

1 tsp (5ml) freshly squeezed lime juice (optional)

Makes 1 cup (approximately ⅓ pint/200ml)

Hot-brew method:

Pour 7oz (200ml) of boiling water per serve over the lemongrass leaves or stalk, plus the ginger, honey, and lime juice (if using), in either the pitcher or teapot (depending on the quantity you are making). Steep for about 5 minutes (or up to 15 minutes, according to your personal taste/the strength of the lemongrass). Let cool and strain into the serving cup(s).

Iced Spring Tonic TEA

Nature provides bitter herbs in spring to restore our bodies after winter. These beautiful herbs fire up our digestive systems, detox our livers and kidneys, kickstart our lymphatic systems, and increase our energy levels. Dandelion (*Taraxacum officinalis*) leaves, chickweed (*Stellaria media*), nettle (*Urtica dioica*) tips, *Mahonia aquifolium* or *M. japonica* flowers, cleavers (*Galium aparine*), violets (*Viola*), and primroses (*Primula vulgaris*) all have such medicinal effects. These plants decontaminate the land (as well as us), so avoid foraging on sites that may be tainted with industrial or agricultural waste. Served over ice with soda or tonic water, this tea is restorative and refreshing.

4 heaped tsp (about a handful) of fresh nettle tips, dandelion leaves, cleavers, mahonia flowers, chickweed, pink/wood sorrel, violet leaves and flowers, and primrose leaves and flowers or 2 heaped tsp of the dried ingredients

7oz (200ml) boiling water

1 tsp (5ml) honey (optional)

Squeeze of fresh lemon (optional)

Handful of ice cubes

Soda or tonic water, to taste

2 dashes of Citrus Bitters (see page 75) or bitters of choice (optional)

Heatproof measuring pitcher, teapot (optional), teaspoon, tea strainer, highball/rocks glass

Makes 1 glass (approximately ⅓ pint/200ml)

To make the spring tonic tea, pick your choice of plants in an area free of dog walkers and never in a cemetery (where there may be arsenic waste). Pick only one or two leaves or flowers from each plant, so you don't harm them. Pick only the first four leaves of very young nettles, using latex gloves to pinch them hard to avoid the sting. You probably won't need gloves to do this once you get used to it—confidence and a firm grip are key—plus nettles lose their sting as soon as they hit boiling water. Free the leaves and flowers of any wildlife, brush off any soil, and tear any leaves into small 1-in (2.5-cm) pieces.

Pour 7oz (200ml) of boiling water per serve over the fresh or dried herbs in either the pitcher or teapot (depending on the quantity you are making). Steep for at least 5 minutes (longer if a more bitter taste is required). Add the teaspoon of honey and squeeze of lemon (if using), while the tea is still piping hot. Strain the tea into a clean pitcher and let cool.

Fill the highball or rocks glass with ice cubes. Pour 4oz (125ml) of the cold tea over the ice and top up with soda or tonic water, according to taste. Add a couple of dashes of bitters, if desired. (Note: Some bitters may contain alcohol, unless glycerin has been used instead.) If you wish, garnish with some of the flowers from your forays. Here, I have used violets and mahonia flowers.

VARIATION

To transform the iced tea into a cocktail, add a measure or two (1–2oz/30–60ml) of alcohol (gin, vodka, and white rum all work well).

Caution: Do not consume more than two teacups of this tea per day, as the herbs are quite potent in early spring. Avoid drinking herbal teas if you are pregnant because many have uterine-stimulating properties, and if you are on blood-thinning medication as they can interact adversely with these medicines.

VIOLET *Tea*

The sight of violet flowers, like bright purple jewels, bursting through the undergrowth in woody areas is a sure sign that spring is on its way. These are wild violets—their sweet scent demands some attention in your libations, but only if you have found large patches of them. You do not want to deprive the bees when pollen is scarce. I am lucky in my area of London, as there are carpets of violets in a patch of local woodland. All species of wild violet are edible and medicinally valuable, but the scent of *Viola odorata* is more accented. You can make this tea using fresh or dried leaves and flowers—the flavor of the blossoms will be stronger if you dry them first (see Drying Herbs, on page 18)—but sometimes it's more fun to have instant gratification from your fresh bounty.

Heatproof measuring pitcher, teapot (optional), teaspoon, tea strainer, serving cup(s)

7oz (200ml) boiling water
2–3 tsp fresh violet flowers and finely torn leaves or 1–2 tsp dried violet flowers and leaves (dried, organic, and unsprayed)
Honey, to taste (optional)
Squeeze of fresh lemon (optional)

Makes 1 cup (approximately ⅓ pint/200ml)

Pour 7oz (200ml) of boiling water per serve over the violet flowers and leaves in either the pitcher or teapot (depending on the quantity you are making). Steep for 5 minutes. Let cool, strain into your serving cup(s), and serve with some honey and lemon (if using).

Both the leaves and flowers of violets are a medicinal and nutritional powerhouse—the leaves are bitter, but the flowers are sweet and tangy. They are loaded with vitamins A and C. In fact, two small violet leaves fulfill our daily requirement of vitamin C! As far back as 1885, a study showed that the leaves, if collected in spring, contain twice as much vitamin C as the same weight of oranges and more than twice the amount of vitamin A, gram for gram, as spinach. They were traditionally used as a blood purifier to be consumed at the end of winter to stimulate the lymphatic glands, eliminate toxins, and generally boost our immune systems and energize us for spring. The other great thing about violets is their color. They produce a gorgeous purple drink that turns cerise when mixed with an acid... all very cool!

Pickled CHERRY BLOSSOM *Tea*

This beautiful recipe doubles up as a delicious tea and a gorgeous garnish. In Japan, the brief blossoming of the Japanese cherry (*Prunus serrulata*) is celebrated with a profusion of teas, cocktails, and related rituals. This traditional recipe was developed over generations to preserve the unique flavor of cherry blossom—known as sakura in Japan—through the year. Sakura tea (which usually also includes rice in Japan) is a specialty served at weddings and other special occasions. The tea has a delicate, salty, sweet, fragrant, and woody flavor. Of course, you need to wash off the salt before using it in either a tea or, as we do at the Midnight Apothecary, as a beautiful garnish in The Cherry Blossom (see page 104), where it will unfurl in your cocktail creation. It is important to pick the blossom at the late-bud stage, or half open at the latest, as you want the buds to unfurl as they hit the hot water, and this is also when they have the most flavor. I try to pick the brightest pink blossom because the color leaches out slightly anyway.

2 cups (about two large handfuls) of fresh, bright pink cherry blossoms, at either bud or half-bloom stage

6 tbsp sea salt

3oz (90ml) Ume plum vinegar

Paper towel

Large ceramic or glass bowl (or pickling crock if you have one)

Large plate

Heavy weight (such as a large pebble or paperweight)

Sealable, airtight glass jar (as used for jellies and jams), sterilized (see page 24)

Fine sieve

Baking paper and baking sheet

Makes enough for approximately 30 teas

Remove any wildlife, stalks, or other debris from the blossoms, and rinse them in water. Carefully lay the blossoms on some paper towel to dry thoroughly.

Once the blossoms are dry, place them in a large bowl, pour the salt over them, and gently mix to ensure they are all coated (try not to bruise the petals).

Place a large plate over the blossoms, followed by a heavy weight (this needs to be at least three times heavier than the flowers), then leave for 2 days. The combination of salt and weight should extract all the liquid from the blossoms. Shake free of salt and place the blossoms in the sterilized glass jar.

Pour over the vinegar, ensuring the blossoms are completely submerged. Seal the jar and then leave in a cool, dark place for 3 days.

Strain the blossoms through a fine sieve and place carefully on a baking sheet lined with baking paper. You can either let the blossoms dry naturally in the sun or put them in the oven at about 160°F (70°C). If you dry the blossoms in the oven, check them regularly—they should be completely dry, but not burnt! Transfer the blossoms to the jar (making sure you wash, dry, and sterilize this again first) and store them in the dark where they will last indefinitely.

SAKURA TEA

To make a cup of sakura tea (well, the simplified Western version!), take one pickled blossom and soak it in a cup of hot water for about 5 minutes, to remove the salt. Reserve the cup of salted water. Place the blossom in a clean teacup, pour over fresh hot water, and use a spoon to add the salt-flavored water according to taste.

The CHERRY BLOSSOM

This cocktail is a celebration of the cherry, from bud to fruit. It is a long, low-alcohol, spring sipper. The taste of cherry is brought to you in five ways—through the tea, the cordial, the soda, the actual fruit, and the blossom (if you add a bloom to the glass). The magnolia brings ginger and acid sweetness to balance it all out in a delicious drink. You can, of course, omit the sake altogether if you'd prefer the drink to be non-alcoholic.

Tools: **Tea strainer, mixing glass, barspoon/long spoon, hawthorne strainer**

Glass: **Highball**

Ice: **Cubes**

Garnish: **Couple of cherries**

2oz (60ml) **Pickled Cherry Blossom Tea (see page 102)**

2oz (60ml) **Junmai sake**

¾oz (20ml) **Cherry Blossom and Flowering Currant Cordial (see page 70)**

¼oz (7ml) **Magnolia Flower Vinegar (see page 81)**

1oz (30ml) **Wild Sour Cherry and Flowering Currant Soda (see page 80)**

Serves 1

Make some Pickled Cherry Blossom Tea, as described on page 103, but use 3 pickled blossoms per glass and let the tea cool completely before building your cocktail. Strain the blossoms and, if you wish, place one at the bottom of the highball glass. Fill the highball glass with ice.

Fill a mixing glass two-thirds of the way up with ice and add the cold Pickled Cherry Blossom Tea, sake, Cherry Blossom and Flowering Currant Cordial, and Magnolia Flower Vinegar. Stir vigorously to cool the drink thoroughly. Strain into the highball glass and top with Wild Sour Cherry and Flowering Currant Soda. Garnish with a couple of cherries.

BONFIRE OF THE
Vani-Teas

Campari is one of those drinks with a secret recipe that no one has seriously been able to replicate. It is packed full of bitter citrus and herby notes which, while giving you prominent bitterness, also provide a sweetness that hits your palate as soon as you sip. I love it and wouldn't have a clue how to replicate it. However, the Pineapple Sage and Scented Geranium Tea (see page 96) combines well with the Campari, plus a great slug of gin. In this case, it's all really just a vehicle for showing off a great-looking, delicious-tasting blossom of pineapple sage (*Salvia elegans*).

2oz (60ml) gin
½oz (15ml) Pineapple Sage and Scented Geranium Tea (see page 96)
½oz (15ml) Campari

Simply stir all the ingredients over ice in the mixing glass and strain into the Martini glass. Garnish with the sprig of flowering pineapple sage.

Tools: **Mixing glass, barspoon/long spoon, hawthorne strainer**
Glass: **Martini**
Ice: **Cubes**
Garnish: **Flowering pineapple sage sprig**

Serves 1

Pineapple sage reaches a height of about 5ft (1.5m) and blooms continuously from early fall/autumn into late winter, like a giant bonfire. Very apt.

LEMONGRASS LEAFTINI

Mocktail

Lemongrass combines beautifully with cooling cucumber to provide a refreshing, aromatic, and elegant mocktail. Note that the Citrus Bitters contain alcohol, but are an optional addition and you will only be using a few drops.

1 unpeeled cucumber

3oz (90ml) cooled Lemongrass Tea (see page 99)

2 tsp (10ml) freshly squeezed lime juice

1 tsp (5ml) heather Honey Syrup, (see page 16, optional)

2 splashes of Citrus Bitters, (see page 75, optional)

Tools: **Sharp knife, chopping board, juicer or food processor/blender, fine-mesh strainer and cheesecloth/muslin (optional), wide-mouthed pitcher (optional), cocktail shaker and strainer**

Glass: **Martini**

Ice: **Rocks**

Garnish: **Borage flower and a fresh lemongrass leaf wrapped around a spear of ginger or a lemongrass stalk**

Serves 1

Roughly chop the cucumber, then process it in a juicer or food processor/blender. If you've used a food processor/blender, you will need to strain the purée through a fine-mesh strainer and cheesecloth/muslin into a wide-mouthed pitcher, to extract the juice. You will need 2oz (60ml) of juice, per serve. Refrigerate the cucumber juice until you serve. Fill the cocktail shaker two-thirds of the way up with ice. Add the cooled tea and cucumber and lime juices, as well as the Honey Syrup and Citrus Bitters (if using). Cover and shake for 20 seconds. Strain into a Martini glass and add your choice of garnish.

BOOZY LEMONGRASS AND CUCUMBER LEAFTINI

To make an alcoholic version, follow the ingredient quantities and directions for the Lemongrass Leaftini Mocktail, but use 2oz (60ml) of Lemongrass Tea and 1½oz (40ml) of cucumber juice, then add 1oz (30ml) of lemongrass-infused vodka or gin. You can make this by infusing 3 fresh lemongrass leaves in a 700 or 750ml bottle of vodka or gin for 3 days. If you don't have any lemongrass leaves, the drink is still delicious simply with the vodka or gin.

VARIATION

If you would like to serve this lemongrass mocktail or cocktail long, fill a highball or large rocks glass with ice, pour in your mix, then top with soda or tonic water. Garnish with a slice of lime, some Thai basil leaves, a cucumber spear and/or a lemongrass leaf/stalk.

"TRUE TEA" TIPPLES

As I mentioned earlier, "true teas" are made from the leaves of the evergreen shrub *Camellia sinensis*, which is more usually known as the tea plant or tea shrub. The most common type of true tea is black tea, but green and white teas are both growing in popularity, due to their greater health-giving properties. The difference between these teas lies in the processing methods used to produce them—black tea, for example, is more oxidized than green, white, and oolong teas; it also has a stronger flavor and a great astringency. The recipes in this section use a variety of different teas, including green teas and more familiar black teas such as Earl Grey and Lapsang Souchong.

LEMONGRASS, PINEAPPLE WEED, and Szechuan Teagroni

The classic bittersweet gorgeousness of a Negroni can benefit from the tannins found in tea (in addition to the Campari and vermouth), to give it added complexity and dryness. If you want a bit of smokiness too, this is where Lapsang Souchong, a black tea, can lend a powerful hand. To balance this cocktail with more sweet herbaceousness, the Lemongrass Tea packs a powerful floral, citrusy, ginger kick, the pineapple weed (*Matricaria discoidea*) brings further unmistakable pineapple sweet notes, while the Szechuan pepper adds another layer of popping zing. The Citrus Bitters provide a final hint of sweetness and aromatics to send this drink off to heaven.

pineapple weed

Tools: **Teaspoon, teacup, muddler or wooden spoon, tea strainer, mixing glass, barspoon/long spoon, hawthorne strainer, vegetable peeler**

Glass: **Rocks**

Ice: **Cubes**

Garnish: **Lemongrass stalk and/or leaf and orange zest**

1 level tsp loose-leaf Lapsang Souchong tea

1oz (30ml) dry gin, such as London Dry

5 pineapple weed flowerheads

1oz (30ml) Wild Dry Vermouth (see page 55) or sweet vermouth

1oz (30ml) Campari

3 Szechuan peppercorns

1oz (30ml) Lemongrass Tea (see page 99)

2 splashes of Citrus Bitters (see page 75)

Serves 1

Add the teaspoon of tea to the teacup and pour over the gin. Crush the pineapple weed flowerheads slightly with the handle of a wooden spoon or a muddler, and add to the cup. After a couple of hours in such a concentrated infusion, they should start to give up some of their delightful pineapple flavor. Leave to infuse for 2 hours. Use the tea strainer to strain the tea and pineapple weed from the gin.

Fill a mixing glass two-thirds of the way up with ice. Add the infused gin, wild/sweet vermouth, Campari, Szechuan peppercorns, Lemongrass Tea, and Citrus Bitters. Stir for 30 seconds until condensation appears on the outside of the glass. Fill a rocks glass with either one large ice cube or two regular cubes. Strain the mix into the glass using the hawthorne strainer. Add the lemongrass stalk or leaf. Peel a 1-in (2.5-cm) piece of zest from an orange, squeeze the peel side of the zest around the rim of the glass to release the essential oils, then drop the zest into the glass.

WINDFALL *Punch*

This is a complex party drink that can be served either hot or cold to bring autumnal, warming notes to your special occasion. The apple brandy and dry cider are natural bedfellows, and also work surprisingly well with the sherry. The Kumquat, Thyme, Cinnamon, and Honey Syrup gives this punch a touch of citrus-y, warming sweetness, while the black tea provides an extra tannic quality to make this a complex, dryer drink. If you can find Spanish cider (known as Sidra), then go for it. It is fermented naturally with the natural yeast found in apples, without added sugars and sweeteners, and is usually still, not sparkling. It tends to have quite a yeasty character and a dry finish, which will be balanced by the apple brandy, kumquats, and honey. Without the Spanish cider, however, this is still quite a dry punch.

Tools: Heatproof measuring pitcher, strainer, large punch bowl, barspoon/long spoon, large nonreactive saucepan (if you wish to warm the punch), ladle

Glasses: **Punch cups or teacups**

Ice: **Large cubes (the larger the better, as you don't want the ice to melt too quickly)**

Garnish: **Apple slices, cinnamon stick, kumquats and/or thyme sprigs**

10oz (300ml) strong black tea

15oz (450ml) Porcini-infused Amontillado Sherry (see page 62)

5oz (150ml) apple brandy, such as Calvados

5oz (150ml) freshly squeezed lemon juice

5oz (150ml) Kumquat, Thyme, Cinnamon, and Honey Syrup (see page 72)

1 liter bottle of dry cider

20 dashes of Becky's Pear, Quince, and Apple Windfall Bitters (see page 77, optional)

Makes about 10 to 15 servings

Make the strong black tea by infusing 5 teabags in boiling water in the pitcher and letting cool before straining. Add the strained tea to the punch bowl, along with all the other ingredients, and stir thoroughly to combine. If you are drinking the punch chilled, refrigerate for at least 2 hours and add large ice cubes just before serving. Simply ladle the punch into small cups and garnish with slices of apple, a cinnamon stick, and kumquats/sprigs of thyme.

To serve the punch hot, simply pour all the ingredients into a large, nonreactive saucepan and warm through until just below boiling point (don't boil the liquid) before ladling into heatproof cups.

The word "punch" is derived from *panch*, which is the Sanskrit word for "five," because the drink was originally made with five ingredients: alcohol, sugar, lemon, water, and tea or spices. The drink was brought from India to England by sailors and employees of the British East India Company in the early 17th century.

For a traditional punch, there is a rhyme from Barbados that provides a basic guideline for the measurements: "One of sour, two of sweet, three of strong, and four of weak."

It is often the tannins present in strong-brewed, double-strength Assam or Ceylon black teas that necessitate the use of sweet elements in a tea punch. Instead of using refined sugar, consider using fruit juice, yacón syrup, soda, raw honey, or sweet herbs to provide part of the sweet element instead. You can also reduce the sweetness of punch by replacing one of the sweet elements with a honey rim on the glass dipped in loose tea leaves. Using less astringent, weaker, or green teas, which work with lighter flavors, means you can also add fewer sweeteners.

Tea can also be used as a spice in tea punches—simply use a coffee grinder to produce a fine, powder-like matcha green tea.

LEMONGRASS, JASMINE GREEN TEA,
and Sake Punch

I realize there are a lot of lemongrass tea recipes in this chapter, but I'm using this herb to demonstrate the number of applications one herb can have—whether as a tea or alcoholic infusion, whether hot-brewed or cold, whether combined with a "true tea" or as a tisane, and whether served as a mocktail or cocktail with a variety of spirits. You can apply these ratios and methods to countless other herbs, too.

Not only is the jasmine green tea used in this punch special because it is a "true tea," but the petals also impart a delicate, but very aromatic, fragrance and a touch of sweetness too. But since the jasmine mostly imparts fragrance and only a subtle flavor to the tea, it also mixes easily with other flavors—such as the lemongrass used here. You could try combining it with complementary flavors such as rose or orange, or perhaps other types of lemon like lemon verbena or lemon balm.

Likewise, the sake lends a light, fragrant, and slightly sweet taste to the cocktail. It lets the other flavors shine through. The birch sap brings a deliciously fresh, silky, slightly sweet note to the drink and is packed full of goodies—if you've also let this ferment a little, it will provide your drink with a slightly sour tonic (see the Fermented Birch Sap, on page 130). Birch sap is the perfect mixer to use, as it doesn't crowd out the other subtle flavors. If you can't source any birch sap, simply leave it out and perhaps add a touch of honey at the tea-making stage instead. The Citrus Bitters provide that extra level of citrus sweetness if you want to fully "season" the drink.

Jasmine tea is usually made from green tea. Green tea is one of the healthiest teas you can drink. It has been shown to have more health benefits than black tea since it doesn't go through the same fermentation process, which means its antioxidants are left in their natural state. In addition, green tea may be helpful for naturally regulating levels of insulin. The best jasmine tea is made with real jasmine petals and the highest quality loose-leaf teas. You'll often find that some of the best and most flavorsome jasmine green teas mix tightly rolled, green-tea pearls with the jasmine petals.

jasmine

20 x 1-in (2.5-cm) pieces of
lemongrass fronds or
½ lemongrass stalk

3oz (90ml) boiling water

1 level tsp jasmine green tea leaves
in an infuser or 1 teabag

1 tsp (5ml) raw honey,
to taste (optional)

2oz (60ml) sake

2oz (60ml) birch sap (optional)

2 dashes of Citrus Bitters,
(see page 75, optional)

Tools: **Teapot or large heatproof
measuring pitcher/bowl (if making
a large quantity), teaspoon,
barspoon/long spoon, tea strainer,
large serving pitcher or punch bowl**

Glass: **Rocks/highball or teacup**

Ice: **Cubes**

Garnish: **Lemongrass frond/stalk,
orange segment, and lemon balm or
lemon verbena sprig (optional)**

Serves 1

Place the chopped-up lemongrass fronds or stalk in the teapot or pitcher/bowl and pour over 3oz (90ml) of boiling water. Wait for 1 minute and then add the jasmine green tea leaves (in an infuser) or the teabag. Let steep for 5 minutes. Remove the jasmine infuser or teabag, as you don't want to over-steep green tea. Immediately add the honey (if using), while the water is still hot enough, and stir to combine until the honey has dissolved. About 1 teaspoon of honey per serve is plenty—you may prefer not to use any honey at all, as you already have some sweetness from the birch sap or the jasmine petals themselves. Leave the lemongrass fronds or stalks in the teapot/pitcher/

bowl until the liquid has cooled. Strain the lemongrass from the infusion into the serving pitcher or punch bowl. Add the sake and birch sap (if using) to the mix. Stir gently to combine.

When ready to serve, fill the serving glass with ice. Pour the punch over the ice and garnish with the lemongrass frond/stalk and orange segment. Add two dashes of Citrus Bitters (or other bitters if you have them). Lemongrass fronds have a wonderful aroma as a garnish if they are rubbed or smacked first. If you are using a lemongrass stalk, try also adding a sprig of lemon balm or lemon verbena for the amazing aroma it offers as you sip.

MATCHA *Sour*

Matcha green tea is all the rage and for very good reason. If it is prepared properly and if you use ceremonial-grade matcha, you will experience so many wonderful taste sensations, let alone health benefits. It is rare to be able to taste vegetal, grassy, bitter, sweet, and malty flavors with just one ingredient. The trick seems to be to use the most expensive grade of matcha tea you can afford—for both flavor and color—and to make sure you don't burn it, as this creates an unpleasant bitterness and a duller green color. When mixed with a dry gin, the botanicals blend beautifully. Here, you could also try using bison grass vodka for a similar effect. The basil provides another level of herbal wonder. Use Thai basil for a bit of a kick, or any other herb that takes your fancy. This method could, I suppose, be called cold brew—in fact, it's an instant cold brew... there's no hanging around with this one!

1 level tsp matcha powder (preferably ceremonial-grade)

3oz (90ml) dry gin, such as London Dry

1oz (30ml) heather Honey Syrup (see page 16)

1oz (30ml) freshly squeezed lemon juice or yuzu juice (if you have it)

1 egg white

4 basil leaves

Tools: **Teaspoon, small bowl, egg whisk or chasen (a beautiful bamboo whisk with fine bristles, which is even better, but not essential), cocktail shaker, hawthorne strainer, tea strainer**

Glass: **Martini/coupe (x 2)**

Ice: **Cubes**

Garnish: **Tiny dots of matcha powder or a basil leaf**

Serves 2

Carefully measure 1 level teaspoon of matcha tea into the bowl and pour over the gin. Using the egg whisk or bamboo chasen, whisk the matcha rapidly to blend it with the gin. You want the gin to practically foam, so will need to make some effort here. Fill your cocktail shaker two-thirds of the way up with ice and add the gin/matcha mix, together with the Honey Syrup, lemon/yuzu juice, egg white, and basil leaves—smack the leaves first to release their essential oils. Cover and shake vigorously for at least 20 seconds to ensure the egg emulsifies. Use a hawthorne strainer and tea strainer to double-strain the mix (see page 25) into the glasses. Garnish with a few tiny dots of matcha powder or a basil leaf, and serve immediately.

Matcha green tea is much stronger than regular brewed green tea, because you are consuming the actual leaves of the plant, which have been grown in the shade to provide intense health benefits. This tea significantly increases energy levels over several hours without giving you the caffeine "jitters." The L-theanine component in this tea increases focus and calmness, while reducing stress. It boosts metabolic rates by 35 to 40 percent in regular drinkers, thus facilitating weight loss. And, on a gram per gram basis, ceremonial-grade matcha tea also has 70 times more antioxidants than orange juice, 200 times the antioxidants of apple juice, and nine times the beta-carotene of spinach.

SCOTCH MIST
at Teatime

Earl Grey is a tea blend with a citrus flavor and aroma due to the addition of oil from the rind of the bergamot orange, *Citrus bergamia* or *Citrus* x *aurantium* subsp. *bergamia*. Here I have mixed the tea with Scotch whisky and used some elderflower liqueur and a teaspoon of Honey Syrup to add extra floral and sweet notes. The lemon juice and Citrus Bitters balance it all out to create a really refreshing drink for sipping.

Tools: **Teacup, cocktail shaker, hawthorne strainer**

Glass: **Coupe**

Ice: **Cubes (optional)**

Garnish: **Sprig of heather and some sweet cicely flowers or a small cube of honeycomb on a toothpick (cocktail stick)**

2oz (60ml) cold Earl Grey tea

2oz (60ml) Scotch whisky, of your choice

¼oz (7ml) elderflower liqueur, such as St Germain

⅔oz (20ml) freshly squeezed lemon juice

1 tsp (5ml) heather Honey Syrup (see page 16)

2 splashes of Citrus Bitters (see page 75)

Serves 1

Steep 1 teabag of Earl Grey tea in 2oz (60ml) of hot water in the teacup for 1 hour and let cool. Fill the cocktail shaker two-thirds of the way up with ice. Add all the ingredients, cover, and shake well. Strain the cocktail into a rocks glass filled with ice cubes. Decorate with your choice of garnish.

Liz Knight, forager and maker of extraordinary elixirs (see *Featured Foragers*, on page 166), had me gorging on bergamot flowers in the beautiful garden where we were based for a recent foraging foray in Wales. The fruit used in Earl Grey tea is not related to the herby namesake we were munching on: *Monarda didyma* (see page 31). This is more commonly known as bergamot or bee balm (because of its tendency to attract bees). The only reason it's called bergamot is because it reminded the botanist who discovered it of the citrus aroma of bergamot orange. However, the bee balm flower is utterly delicious and fragrant—tasting like a sweet, bright red, solid version of Earl Grey tea. If you stick a fresh leaf of bee balm in tea, it will help to relieve insomnia, menstrual pain, nausea, and flatulence. A fresh leaf infused with China tea will produce the flavor of Earl Grey tea.

CHAPTER 6
CULTURED DRINKS

I hadn't really appreciated how important fermented drinks and foods, and the beneficial bacteria they contain, are to our gut health and overall wellbeing. Our ancestors understood the value of these fermented products, as do modern communities that rely on unprocessed food. In contrast, today's sanitized diets and obsession with killing bacteria have left many of us with poor intestinal health. Whereas in the past we would have enjoyed fermented vegetables out of necessity, because there were no refrigerators and freezers to store unseasonal food, science is only now uncovering the vast ecosystem of yeasts and bacteria that are so vital to our immune and digestive systems.

My "adventures in mold" and healthy forays down a "cultured" road have yielded some great mocktails and cocktails that might just fit the bill for you too. This chapter explains how to make cultured or fermented drinks such as kombucha, kefir, and kvass—often using the simplest of ingredients and equipment—to help diversify your gut bacteria. Aside from their abundant health benefits, which include increased energy levels, these fermented drinks also enable us to play around with their complex flavors, depth, fizz, and sparkle!

ADVENTURES IN MOLD

The recipes in this chapter are intended as a brief introduction to the art of making cultured drinks with a wealth of health benefits. Many of these drinks can also be used as an ingredient in a selection of delicious mocktails and cocktails.

KOMBUCHA

Kombucha is a fermented sweetened tea or tea vinegar with its origins some 2,000 years ago in East Asia, where it was known as the "immortal health elixir." Not only does this tangy, slightly sweet tea bring joy to mocktails and cocktails, it is also bursting with health benefits. Indeed, researchers studying the benefits of kombucha report positive effects on liver detoxification, increased energy, better digestion, improved mood, the elimination of candida (a yeast infection), improved nutrient assimilation, better immune health, benefits to joints, cancer prevention, and weight loss.

Fermenting kombucha

For kombucha, you simply make a tea (usually black, though you can also use green and herbal teas) and sweeten it with about a cup of sugar per gallon. The kombucha is fermented using a culture called a SCOBY (Symbiotic Colony of Bacteria and Yeast), or mother, which you can find in health food stores or online. You may even be "gifted" a SCOBY by a fellow kombucha-maker. The first fermentation takes about 7–21 days, depending on the type of flavor you want. Less time means a less sour and complex drink, while leaving your kombucha for longer results in more depth and a vinegary taste.

Adding sugar to tea might go against the grain of this book, but this is the one time I use organic cane sugar. Quite simply, without sugar, kombucha can't ferment. Rest assured, though: the sugar is used to feed the yeasts, which then feed the bacteria, and not you. They convert almost all the sugar into carbon dioxide (to give a nicely carbonated effect) and ethanol (alcohol)—but only around 1 percent—leaving just 2g of sugar per 8oz (240ml) of kombucha. This is less than half the amount of natural sugar in carrot juice! Plus, if that wasn't good enough news, the resulting kombucha also contains probiotics, beneficial acids and enzymes, and B and other vitamins.

If you undertake a second (or double) fermentation, you can also add a host of delicious fruits and other botanical ingredients to create a hugely healthy, grown-up, fruity and/or floral fizzy soda.

KEFIR

Kefir is another fermented probiotic drink. It uses "grains" (these are not real grains; this is just what they look like), which are another type of SCOBY, to digest sugar to produce probiotics. All versions of kefir—water kefir and milk kefir—pack a powerful bacterial punch.

Water kefir doesn't contain caffeine, or the powerful enzymes and acids of kombucha, but it wins out on the amount of beneficial bacteria it provides and how quick

water kefir grains

milk kefir grains

it is to make. While water kefir tastes milder than milk kefir, it only requires a couple of days' fermentation. Also, because you are using water, fruit juice, or coconut water as the base, it's dairy-free, grain-free, and vegan. Although sweet, it's also a little bland and so provides the perfect background for other flavorings. These can be added during a second fermentation, so you will have a finished kefir in under a week.

Milk kefir is traditionally made with cows' or goats' milk, but you can also use coconut and nut milks. As the bacteria consume most of the lactose in the dairy milk, it can be drunk by most lactose-intolerant people. The fermented milk also increases the bioavailability of nutrients such as phosphorus, calcium, and magnesium. You are left with a slightly carbonated drink with the consistency of thin yogurt. Coconut milk kefir makes a great base for a piña colada, whether virgin or alcoholic. It is extremely easy to make—see my recipe on page 128.

KVASS

This lacto-fermented drink originates from Russia and was once the most common drink across every strata of Russian society. It was made by fermenting stale rye sourdough bread, but you can use beets (beetroot) or other vegetables. Maybe this doesn't sound that

appealing, but try the Beet Kvass (see page 125) and see if you don't enjoy its earthy saltiness. Kvass is very hydrating and helps restore the body's balance of electrolytes—without the modern-day sweeteners, preservatives, and other processed chemicals found in today's sports drinks. Kvass aids digestion and is a delicious drink that alkalizes the blood, cleanses the liver, and boosts energy levels.

OTHER FERMENTED DRINKS

For centuries, people have made naturally fermented "sodas" from sweetened herbal teas or fruit juices. These are packed with probiotics and beneficial enzymes that are a far cry from commercially available sweet sodas and sports drinks. Ginger ale is just one naturally fizzy example that combines the benefits of probiotics and enzymes with the health properties of ginger—see pages 132–33, for my Homemade Ginger Ale recipe.

Birch sap is another popular health drink. In fact, people in cold countries have drunk birch sap as a health tonic for centuries. It contains fructose, glucose, a small amount of sucrose, fruit acids, amino acids, as well as a wealth of vitamins and minerals. It works out at only 21 kilojoules (5kcal) per 3½oz (100ml), so it's super-healthy. It can either be drunk on its own (see Fermented Birch Sap, page 130) or incorporated into mocktails/cocktails.

SIMPLE KOMBUCHA

The process of making kombucha is simple. It just takes patience. Importantly, you need filtered or distilled water, as the chlorine, fluoride, and other chemicals in most tap water will kill the yeasts and bacteria. Even the minerals in mineral and spring water can harm the SCOBY over time, so always use filtered or distilled water for the best results.

This recipe requires sugar. I use organic cane sugar. Brown (turbinado) sugar is harder for the kombucha to break down and changes the color of the finished drink quite considerably, but is fine to use if you prefer. You can also use honey, but don't be tempted to use raw honey because the bacteria it contains may disturb the SCOBY balance and lead to a dominance of harmful bacteria. Also make sure you use the full amount of sugar suggested in the recipe; otherwise you will inhibit the kombucha's development.

You will need to decide whether to make one large batch of kombucha or to go for a continuous brew. As the name suggests, the first method involves brewing the kombucha in one batch and then re-starting the process each time by using the SCOBY "baby" (which forms alongside the mother SCOBY every one or two brews) and some of the liquid from a previous batch.

Alternatively, you can have a continuous brew—which is the method I describe here—by removing only some of the liquid each time and replacing it with the same amount of freshly brewed sweetened tea. This speeds up the brewing time, reduces the risk of molds and other

Caution: People who are sugar-intolerant should consider fermenting kombucha for 3 weeks or longer, to reduce the sugar levels still further. Those who have a compromised immunity also need to be careful when consuming kombucha, as there is a possibility of growing harmful bacteria during the fermentation process. Following good hygiene practices, including sterilizing all equipment (see page 24), when brewing kombucha is crucial and should mitigate these risks.

forms of contamination, as the bacteria and yeasts get more balanced, and also produces a wider array of bacteria and other beneficial nutrients in the final product. For a continuous brew, you will need a larger glass container with a spigot to draw off the brewed kombucha, leaving behind enough mature brew to continue the process.

When brewing, use inert, food-safe equipment made from materials such as glass. Kombucha will leach toxins from plastic and metal equipment, and so these materials must never come into contact with the SCOBY. I like to use a 1½-gallon (5.5-liter) glass container with a spigot and I always make sure that at least half the liquid is left at all times. The spigot needs to be made of BPA-free plastic, stainless steel, or wood and also be detachable for cleaning afterward. I use a clean cotton dishtowel and rubber band over the container. This allows oxygen into the brew for the ferment, but has a close enough weave to keep out fruit flies and other foreign bodies (cheesecloth has too open a weave).

HOW TO GET A SCOBY

I got my first SCOBY from Kim, the photographer of this book. She gave me a "baby" SCOBY and one or two cups of brewed kombucha starter liquid. If you haven't got a Kim in your life, you can order a SCOBY and the starter liquid from a reputable online supplier (see *Resources*, pages 172–73). You'll need one SCOBY and 1 cup (250ml) of starter liquid for each gallon (3.5 liters) of kombucha you plan to brew.

1 gallon (3.5 liters) filtered water (free of chlorine, chloramines, and fluoride)

6 black teabags or 1–2 tbsp loose black or green tea (feel free to add herbal teas and/or the dried petals/buds of plants such as hibiscus or elderflower)

1 cup (200g) organic cane sugar

1 large kombucha SCOBY (rehydrate this first if you bought it dehydrated)

1–2 cups (250–500ml) starter liquid (either from a previous kombucha brew or bought with the kombucha SCOBY)

Fresh fruit (such as berries), fruit juice, citrus juice, citrus peel, or herbs of choice, for flavoring (see Method for quantities)

Large saucepan

Nonmetal stirring utensil (plastic is fine), sterilized (see page 24)

1½-gallon (5.5-liter) food-safe brewing jar with a spigot, sterilized (see page 24)

Fermentation cover (such as a clean piece of cotton/closely woven dishtowel/T-shirt or coffee filter) and rubber band

Drinking straw

Wide-mouthed glass jar(s) with plastic screw-top lid(s) or bottle(s) with flip-top cap(s), sterilized (see page 24), for each "second-ferment" flavor

Makes approximately 1 gallon (3.5 liters)

To make the sweet tea, heat the filtered water in the saucepan, add the teabags/tea leaves and sugar, and bring to a boil, stirring to ensure the sugar doesn't form crystals at the bottom of the pan. Remove from the heat immediately and allow the tea to steep for about 5–10 minutes (according to taste).

Remove the teabags/tea leaves and allow the sweetened tea to cool to room temperature—any warmer and you will kill the yeasts and bacteria in your SCOBY, so be patient! Pour the cooled tea into the sterilized jar. Wash your hands thoroughly and add the SCOBY and starter liquid to the jar. Cover the jar with your choice of fermentation cover and secure with a rubber band.

Put the jar in a warm place with a fairly stable temperature—such as a cupboard or countertop away from direct sunlight and excessive heat or cold. In warm summers or heated kitchens, a brew time of 7–21 days is fine. In colder temperatures, up to 3 weeks can be better. Smaller batch sizes can be ready in under a week, while 2 gallons (7.5 liters) can sometimes take a month. Taste the kombucha periodically with a straw to test whether it's ready. It should taste tart and earthy, but slightly sweet. You now have kombucha!

To carbonate your kombucha, and make it more flavorsome and slightly sweeter, you will need to do a second fermentation. This simply means drawing off some of the brew into the sterilized jar(s) or bottle(s) and adding some fresh fruit, fruit juice, citrus juice, citrus peel, or herbs—just use whatever botanical ingredients

you wish to flavor your kombucha with. A ratio of 80 percent kombucha to 20 percent additional ingredient is about right.

Put the lids or caps tightly on the jars or bottles and leave at room temperature for 2–3 days to carbonate. To release the pressure from the carbon dioxide, "burp" your second-brew kombucha daily by slowly unscrewing the lids (or flipping the caps). If you are worried about the jars or bottles exploding, store them in a secure box or cupboard. Once the kombucha is carbonated, store in the refrigerator between uses. Consume within 3 months.

Note: Don't forget to top up your continuous kombucha brewing jar with more cooled sweet tea to keep the cycle going.

GINGER, LEMON, AND LAVENDER
Kombucha

This recipe demonstrates how easy it is to use various botanical ingredients to enhance a basic kombucha. Feel free to experiment with whatever flavor combinations appeal to you. Here I have used ginger, lavender, and lemon. Try using this delicious kombucha in a Hot Strawberry Fizz (see page 163).

4 cups (1 liter) Simple Kombucha (see page 122)
1 tbsp culinary-grade lavender buds
1 tbsp freshly grated ginger
3-in (7.5-cm) piece of lemon zest, white pith removed
Freshly squeezed juice of ½ lemon

1-quart (1-liter) wide-mouthed jar, with plastic screwtop lid, sterilized (see page 24)
Lemon juicer
Fine-mesh strainer and muslin/cheesecloth or coffee filter
Sealable presentation bottle(s), sterilized (see page 24)

Makes approximately 1 quart (1 liter)

Make the kombucha following the method for a Simple Kombucha (see page 123). At the second-ferment stage, simply add the lavender buds, grated ginger, and lemon zest and juice to the sterilized jar and pour in the kombucha. Seal the jar tightly and store at room temperature. "Burp" the kombucha once a day for 24–48 hours until you are happy with the flavor and level of carbonation. Fine-strain the kombucha (see page 25) into sterilized presentation bottle(s) and store in the refrigerator. Consume within 3 months.

To serve, fill a highball glass with ice and pour in your kombucha. For an alcoholic hit, top up with some sparkling wine or champagne.

lavender

BEET *Kvass*

This fermented beet (beetroot) juice is packed with probiotics and enzymes. It makes a salty and earthy contribution to a virgin or alcoholic Bloody Mary—try using it as a substitute for tomato juice in the Regal Mary Mocktail (see page 148). Alternatively, mix it with an earthy spirit, such as mezcal or tequila, to make a delicious cocktail.

1-quart (1-liter) wide-mouthed jar, sterilized (see page 24)

Fermentation cover (such as a clean piece of cotton/closely woven dishtowel/T-shirt or coffee filter) and rubber band

Fine-mesh strainer and muslin/ cheesecloth or coffee filter

Sealable presentation bottle(s), sterilized (see page 24)

2 large or 4 small organic beets (beetroot), washed (peeled first if non-organic)

¼ cup (50ml) whey (the strained liquid from full-fat plain yogurt) or lacto-fermented pickle juice (from a commercial jar of sauerkraut)

1 tbsp sea salt

1 quart (1 liter) filtered (chlorine-free) water

Makes approximately 1 quart (1 liter)

Chop the beet/beetroot into ½-in (1-cm) cubes and put in the sterilized jar. Add the whey or pickle juice and salt, then pour in the filtered water. Cover with the fermentation cover and secure with a rubber band. Leave at room temperature for 2 days in a cupboard or on a countertop away from direct sunlight until the mix has fermented. Fine-strain the kvass (see page 25) into a wide-mouthed pitcher, funnel into the sterilized presentation bottle(s), seal, and store in the refrigerator. Consume within 3 months.

Water KEFIR

Fermented water kefir is relatively quick to make and you can have your first kefir to drink within 72 hours. This is an inexact science, though, as the time it takes to make your water kefir will depend on whether you had to rehydrate the kefir grains first, as well as on the season and ambient temperature. If you are happy to wait for a second fermentation, you can add secondary flavors such as fresh ginger, fresh or dried fruit (like pineapple, figs, cherries, and raisins), or garden or foraged spices. Avoid using citrus juice for a second ferment, as this leads to stringy, yeasty additions that I do not feel lend themselves well to mocktails. However, fresh citrus juice added immediately to your drinking glass with the kefir water is delicious—a healthy lemonade! You can also use water kefir in the Regal Mary Mocktail (see page 148).

You will need some water kefir cultures (also called water kefir grains). These are another form of SCOBY, but have a grainy, cauliflower-like appearance. As for the choice of water, it must be free of chlorine and fluoride, but contain the minerals found in mineral or spring water (which are lacking in filtered or distilled water). If you can't get hold of mineral or spring water, boil some tap water to remove the chlorine and let cool.

water kefir grains

4 tbsp organic unrefined cane sugar

4 cups (1 liter) cool spring or mineral water

3 tbsp (45g) hydrated water kefir grains

Fruit juice, fresh or dried fruit (such as raisins), herbs, or spices of choice, for flavoring (see Method for quantities)

2 x 1-quart (1-liter) wide-mouthed, sealable jars, sterilized (see page 24)

Nonmetal stirring utensil (plastic is fine), sterilized (see page 24)

Fermentation cover (such as a clean piece of cotton/closely woven dishtowel/T-shirt or coffee filter) and rubber band

Plastic or bamboo sieve (avoid metal utensils)

Makes approximately 1 quart (1 liter)

Dissolve the sugar in a small amount of hot water in one of the sterilized jars. When the sugar has dissolved, fill the jar with the cool spring/mineral water. Make sure the water is at room temperature (about 72°F/22°C) and no warmer. Add the water kefir grains, cover the jar with the fermentation cover, and secure with a rubber band. Leave the jar in a warm cupboard (preferably at 70–75°F/21–24°C) or on a countertop out of direct sunlight for 24–48 hours. The longer you leave the kefir, the more sugar will be consumed and the healthier it becomes. Any longer than 48 hours and you risk starving the grains. Stirring the grains regularly can speed up the fermentation process. When the kefir is fermented to your liking, remove the kefir grains by straining the kefir through the sieve into the second sterilized jar. Screw on the airtight lid. You now have water kefir.

To carbonate the kefir and add flavor, you'll need to do a second fermentation for another 1–3 days. Using a ratio of 80 percent water kefir to 20 percent additional juice, add your favorite fruit juice to the water kefir you've just strained. Also feel free to experiment with fresh or dried fruits, herbs, or spices at this stage. Seal the jar tightly with the airtight lid and leave in a cupboard or on the countertop away from direct sunlight for 1–3 days before drinking or refrigerating. Consume within 3 months.

WATER KEFIR GRAINS

As soon as your water kefir grains arrive, rinse them in spring or mineral water and keep them in fresh spring or mineral water with some added sugar, as they need to feed to survive. They may take a few days to get going if you've bought them online, especially if the weather has been cold.

Simply drink your water kefir as it is or serve with some additional fruit juice, iced herbal tea, or citrus juice and ice. Alcohol is optional!

COCONUT WATER KEFIR

You can make Coconut Water Kefir simply by replacing the spring or mineral water in the Water Kefir recipe with coconut water. Try using this in the Coconut Water Kefir Strawberry Cosmo (see page 141).

Cow's Milk KEFIR

Well-fermented milk kefir has quite a strong, sour taste and can even be slightly carbonated. Shorter fermentation times result in a milder flavor. A few people have an intolerance to milk kefir, so I have only given a small-batch recipe here—you can always multiply out the ratios if you decide it's to your liking. I have also provided a recipe for Coconut Milk Kefir, in case that is more suitable for you.

1 tsp milk kefir grains

1 cup (250ml) organic whole milk (preferably non-homogenized)

1-quart (1-liter) wide-mouthed jar, sterilized (see page 24)

Wooden spoon or chopstick, sterilized (see page 24)

Fermentation cover (such as a clean piece of cotton/closely woven dishtowel/T-shirt or coffee filter) and rubber band

Drinking straw

Plastic or bamboo sieve (avoid metal utensils)

Wide-mouthed glass or plastic pitcher (not metal), sterilized (see page 24)

Sealable presentation bottle, sterilized (see page 24)

Makes approximately ½ pint (250ml)

Put the milk kefir grains in the sterilized jar, pour in the milk, and gently stir with the wooden spoon or chopstick. Cover with the fermentation cover and secure with a rubber band (the gas needs to be able to escape). Store in a cupboard or on a countertop out of direct sunlight. The warmer the location—ideally 72°F (22°C)—the quicker your kefir will ferment. Taste with a straw after 12 hours. Stir once a day to speed up the fermentation process.

The kefir should be ready within 48 hours. Your very first batch is unlikely to taste great, but don't be disheartened: the balance of yeasts and lactobacillus will improve with each batch.

Once you have a slightly thickened kefir that has just started to separate into thick curds and liquid whey, strain the contents through the sieve, stirring gently, into a wide-mouthed pitcher and then funnel into the sterilized presentation bottle. Seal and store in the refrigerator, where the kefir will ripen slowly and ferment further. Consume within 1 week.

COCONUT MILK KEFIR

Coconut milk kefir is milder and less tangy than its dairy counterpart. I use a canned organic coconut milk, which has a lusciously rich texture due to its fat content. However, you will still need milk kefir grains when making this kefir to get the fermentation process going.

Follow the instructions for the Cow's Milk Kefir, but use 1½ cups (400ml) of organic coconut milk with 1 tablespoon of milk kefir grains. The fermented coconut milk should be ready in 3 days (rather than 2 days).

Store the kefir in the refrigerator between uses, but note that the milk kefir grains will not survive in coconut milk kefir, as they require the lactose (milk sugar) in dairy milk to thrive. So, you will need to replace the kefir grains regularly if you want to repeat the process. Consume within 1 week.

Try using this kefir in a very grown-up Vegan and Virgin Piña Colada (see page 140).

MILK KEFIR GRAINS

To revive your milk kefir grains if you've bought them online, rinse them gently with fresh milk through a plastic or bamboo sieve. Place them in milk immediately, as they need the lactose (milk sugar) to survive. They may take a few days to get going, especially if the weather is cold.

FERMENTED
Birch Sap

Birch sap is a burst of fresh, silky, slightly sweet, early-spring gorgeousness packed with nutrients that cleanse, detoxify, and boost your liver and kidneys—a very rare combination. You can use birch sap instead of water in mocktails or cocktails, which gives you another joyous mixer for your cocktail cabinet. Try it in the Beet, Cacao Nib, and Yacón Syrup Mocktail (see page 136).

If you don't drink your birch sap straight away, it will start to ferment naturally after a few days—if left on the countertop or even in the refrigerator. And it's this fermented stuff that I am playing with here. To speed up the fermentation process, simply add a handful of raisins to the birch sap. You will be left with a sour tonic that is packed with probiotics. You can also add herbs, fruits, and spices of your choice to enhance the flavor. I use the fermented tonic in the Sea Buckthorn and Fermented Birch Sap Mocktail (see page 145) and the Wild Vermouth and Fermented Birch Sap Cocktail (see page 155).

1-quart (1-liter) wide-mouthed jar, sterilized (see page 24)

Fermentation cover (such as a clean piece of cotton/closely woven dishtowel/T-shirt or coffee filter) and rubber band

Fine-mesh strainer and muslin/ cheesecloth or coffee filter

Sealable presentation bottle(s), sterilized (see page 24)

4 cups (1 liter) fresh birch sap (either store-bought or freshly tapped)

A handful of raisins

Selection of herbs, spices, and fruits of choice, for flavoring

Makes approximately 1 quart (1 liter)

Pour your birch sap into the sterilized jar and add the raisins to speed up the fermentation. Add your choice of herbs, fruits, or spices to enhance the flavor. Cover the jar with the fermentation cover and secure with a rubber band. Leave at room temperature for 2 days. Fine-strain the fermented birch sap (see page 25) into a wide-mouthed pitcher and funnel into the sterilized presentation bottle(s). Keep in the refrigerator and consume within 1 week.

HOW TO TAP BIRCH SAP

For anyone who has not sampled the joys of birch tapping in very early spring, I thoroughly recommend it . All species of birch can be tapped, the most common being the white birch (*Betula alba*) and the silver birch (*Betula pendula*). Alternatively, fresh birch sap is available from some health-food and grocery stores, although you won't enjoy the romance of tapping your own.

1

Wait until temperatures start rising above freezing (early spring in the U.K.) and find a birch tree with a diameter of at least 10in (25cm)—the more branches the tree has, the better the sap will flow.

2

Make a natural tap from a piece of shaved twig for directing the sap into a plastic collecting container (such as a bottle). You can also use food-grade tubing instead of a twig. Find a spot on the trunk, about 3ft (1m) above the ground. Tie the container to the tree at this point and wedge the twig tap or tubing inside so the sap will run into it. (Cover open containers, as the sap will attract insects.)

3

Drive a sharp knife into the tree at an upward angle, just above the collecting container, to a depth of about 1½in (4cm). Create a small flap in the bark and then use the twig tap or tubing to direct the sap into the container. The water-like sap should start flowing and collecting in the container almost immediately. You can leave the container attached to the tree until the flow of sap slows down or starts turning cloudy (which indicates that the window of opportunity has closed). Only tap a maximum of 1 gallon (3.5 liters) of sap—this will take about a day. The birch-tapping season only lasts 2–3 weeks.

4

At the end of the session, carefully remove the twig tap or tubing, and press down hard on the flap of raised birch bark to close the slit as best you can. The birch tree will then do the rest to seal and heal the bark.

Homemade GINGER ALE

Lacto-fermented drinks such as ginger ale are super-healthy because they are packed with probiotics and enzymes. Ginger ale is a great drink to have in your repertoire, as both a mixer and a sipper in its own right. Ginger has been used for thousands of years for everything, from soothing digestive problems and relieving nausea to stimulating the circulatory system and even lowering cholesterol and blood pressure. Due to the short brewing time, ginger ale is alcohol-free. If left for weeks, you would have something a lot more potent. The ginger ale is made in two stages: you create some cultured ginger (or a "ginger bug") first and then combine this with fresh ginger and a few other ingredients. You can also use your ginger bug as a base for other fruit sodas to give them a wonderfully fermented ginger base. That's what they did in the old days! Try using the ginger ale in the Roast Rhubarb, Blood Orange, Sweet Cicely, and Lemongrass Mocktail (see page 139).

STAGE 1: THE GINGER BUG

As with the SCOBY used when making kombucha or a sourdough starter, here you are creating a culture of beneficial bacteria with ginger and sugar.

1½-in (4-cm) piece of peeled ginger, grated or finely chopped, plus extra for feeding the ginger bug (see Method for quantities)

2 tbsp organic cane sugar, plus extra for feeding the ginger bug (see Method for quantities)

1 tsp molasses

2 cups (500ml) filtered (chlorine-free) water

1-quart (1-liter) wide-mouthed, sealable jar, sterilized (see page 24)

Nonmetal spoon (plastic is fine), sterilized (see page 24)

Fermentation cover (such as a clean piece of cotton/closely woven dishtowel/T-shirt or coffee filter) and rubber band

Makes approximately 1 pint (500ml)

Put the ginger, sugar, and molasses in the sterilized jar and add the filtered water. Stir with a nonmetal spoon, cover the jar with the fermentation cover, and secure with a rubber band. Each day, for 5 days, remove the cover, stir, and add 1 tablespoon each of grated ginger and sugar, before replacing the cover and re-securing the rubber band.

The ferment can take up to 8 days, but you'll know when it's ready because the ginger bug will fizz slightly when stirred, appear cloudy, and have a sweet, yeasty odor. Make sure you keep your ginger bug away from other cultures, such as kombucha or kefir, as they can cross-contaminate—4ft (1.2m) is the recommended distance apart.

Once your ginger bug is ready, use it to make some refreshing homemade ginger ale (following the method described in Stage 2, opposite) or, alternatively, leave it to rest (see box on *Resting Your Ginger Bug*).

RESTING YOUR GINGER BUG

I don't have children or pets, so this is the closest I come to having dependents—all my ferments, including my ginger bug, need feeding if I want them to stay alive! You can rest your ginger bug by putting it in the refrigerator and feeding it with 1 tablespoon each of finely chopped ginger and sugar per week. Or, if you want it to start fermenting in earnest for another batch of soda, put it back in the cupboard or on the countertop at room temperature and feed it daily with 1 teaspoon each of finely chopped ginger and sugar.

STAGE 2: THE GINGER ALE

4 cups (1 liter) filtered (chlorine-free) water

1½-in (4-cm) piece of peeled ginger, grated or finely chopped

¼ cup (50g) organic cane sugar

2 tsp molasses

¼ tsp sea salt

¼ cup (50ml) freshly squeezed lemon juice

¼ cup (50ml) Ginger Bug (see Stage 1, left)

Note: To increase the quantity of ginger ale, use ¼ cup (50g) sugar and ¼ cup (50ml) of ginger bug for each 1 quart (1 liter) of water (and adjust the other ingredient amounts accordingly).

Nonreactive pan

Nonmetal spoon (plastic is fine), sterilized (see page 24)

1-quart (1-liter) wide-mouthed, sealable jar, sterilized (see page 24)

Fine-mesh strainer and muslin/ cheesecloth or gold coffee filter

Sealable presentation bottle(s), sterilized (see page 24)

Makes approximately 1 quart (1 liter)

Add 1½ cups (375ml) filtered water, the ginger, sugar, molasses, and sea salt to the pan and bring to a boil, stirring occasionally to ensure the sugar has dissolved. Allow the mix to simmer gently for 5 minutes. Remove from the heat, add the remaining 2½ cups (625ml) of water, and let the mix cool down to room temperature. Add the lemon juice and Ginger Bug.

Funnel the ginger ale into the sterilized jar, seal, upend gently a couple of times to combine, and then leave in a cupboard or on a countertop out of direct sunlight for 2–3 days until you can see signs of carbonation (i.e. bubbles). The ginger ale is ready when it smells of a combination of ginger and yeast, and is a bit fizzy. In the unlikely event that it is looking very fizzy, you need to "burp" the jar to release the pressure to avoid an explosion (see page 123).

Fine-strain the mixture (see page 25) into a wide-mouthed pitcher and funnel into the sterilized presentation bottle(s). Store in the refrigerator and consume within 6 months.

VARIATION

To use your ginger bug to make other fruit or herb sodas, simply use ¼ cup (50ml) of ginger bug per 1 quart (1 liter) of sweetened mix or your chosen fruit juice.

CHAPTER 7
MIXING IT UP

Now that you've grown, foraged, bought, and/or made the seasonal elixirs from previous chapters, it's time to put them together to widen your mocktail and cocktail repertoire. These are just a few ideas, both alcoholic and non-alcoholic, and they combine the best of the earlier recipes into something truly delicious. The idea behind *Chapter 4: Drink or Mix* was to keep things very simple. There are simple ideas in this chapter too, but they involve a few more combinations—some are a bit tea-like, some spritz-y, and some more complex. Part of the fun is in playing around with different flavors and textures (and base spirits if you're opting for booze). From mocktails to light aperitifs, complex cocktails to boozy digestives, enjoy deciding what to mix with what based on what's in season around you, how healthy you want to be, and how boozy you want to go. Have a happy and healthy cocktail hour!

MOCKTAILS

Being without alcohol does not have to mean going without. You have some utterly delicious, refreshing, luxurious, and healthy options in your drinks armory. Here are just a few seasonal treasures that use some of the drink elements from previous chapters.

BEET, CACAO NIB, AND YACÓN SYRUP
Mocktail

Beet (beetroot) and chocolate are natural bedfellows. The cacao nibs give a surprising level of bitterness to this drink, but the beet is naturally sweet. I have suggested using a drop of yacón syrup, mainly for mouth-feel, but this also provides a very pleasant sweetness that pairs well with the other ingredients. The syrup will not discolor the drink because the beet is so dark. I like to top up this mocktail with a dose of birch sap and a dash of sparkling water, but you can just add extra sparkling water if you don't have any birch sap. Ice cubes are used in this drink, as there's no need to keep the beet unctuous... the yacón syrup and other ingredients make this drink interesting for the palate.

Tools: Muddler, cocktail shaker with strainer, tea strainer

Glass: Rocks

Ice: Cubes

Garnish: Nasturtium flower, *Anchusa azurea* **'Lodden Royalist',** **and blackcurrant sage (***Salvia microphylla***) leaf**

1 tsp raw cacao nibs
2oz (60ml) beet (beetroot) juice
2 tsp (10ml) yacón syrup
2oz (60ml) birch sap
2 dashes of Bittermens Xocolatl Mole Bitters (optional)
Splash of sparkling water

Serves 1

Tip the cacao nibs into the bottom of the cocktail shaker. Use the muddler to crush the nibs and release their flavor. Fill the shaker two-thirds of the way up with ice. Add all the other ingredients (except the sparkling water). Shake vigorously, then double-strain (see page 25) into the rocks glass to catch the nibs and add the splash of sparkling water.

Garnish with your choice of herbaceous or spicy flowers and edible greenery. I've used a yellow nasturtium flower, a blackcurrant sage leaf, and a sprig of blue *Anchusa azurea* 'Lodden Royalist.'

ROAST QUINCE, SZECHUAN PEPPER, JUNIPER, AND STAR ANISE *Mocktail*

When there is a seasonal glut of well-paired ingredients, such as quince and Szechuan pepper, it's a shame not to max out their potential in all kinds of foods and drinks. You can roast quince to make a dessert and then use the leftover juices in this mocktail. (Please note the Citrus Bitters contain a tiny amount of alcohol.)

Tools: **Mixing glass, barspoon/ long spoon, strainer**
Glass: **Highball/rocks**
Ice: **Cubes**
Garnish: **Roasted quince segment**

¼ cup (50ml) Roast Quince Juice (see below)

1oz (30ml) apple and rhubarb juice, apple juice, or pear juice (or apple verjuice if you have any)

¼ cup (50ml) sparkling water, birch sap, or tonic water (whichever your prefer)

2 dashes of Citrus Bitters, (see page 75, optional)

Fill the mixing glass two-thirds of the way up with ice, add the Roast Quince Juice and your choice of fruit juice, then stir well to chill down the drink. Strain the mocktail into the serving glass, top up with your choice of sparkling water/birch sap/tonic water, and add the Citrus Bitters (if using). Garnish with a segment of roasted quince.

Serves 1

ROAST QUINCE JUICE

This recipe provides enough juice to make two mocktails.

1 large quince, peeled and cut into slim, ½-in (1-cm) chunks

7 Szechuan peppercorns

7 juniper berries

1 star anise

5oz (150ml) pear or apple juice (or apple verjuice if you have any)

¼ cup (50ml) maple syrup

Freshly squeezed Juice of ½ lemon

3 x 1-in (2.5-cm) pieces of lemon zest

Small roasting pan
Fine-mesh strainer
Measuring pitcher

To roast the quince, preheat the oven to 180°C/350°F/Gas 4. Place the peeled and chopped quince, Szechuan peppercorns, juniper berries, star anise, pear juice, maple syrup, and lemon juice and zest in the roasting pan. Stir well to coat the quince. Roast for 30 minutes, stirring occasionally to make sure nothing sticks to the pan. Remove and let cool before straining ⅓ cup (100ml) of the cooled liquid into the pitcher (see page 25), ready for making your mocktails.

If you make some Quince Vodka with Szechuan Pepper, Star Anise, and Juniper Berries (see page 52), try shaking it over ice with a tiny drop of maple syrup and a squeeze of lemon and pour it into a sherry glass. To garnish, dry a segment of quince in an oven with a very low setting (for 1 hour at 140°F/60°C) or in a dehydrator (for 10 hours at 140°F/60°C degrees). Dip it in lemon juice first to prevent browning.

ROAST RHUBARB, BLOOD ORANGE, SWEET CICELY, AND LEMONGRASS *Mocktail*

Like the mocktail opposite, this recipe involves straining off the delicious juices from a potential dessert, letting them cool, and sticking them in a glass. I have given two options for the mixer: you can either use Homemade Ginger Ale and sparkling water or, if you have a juicer, try topping up the drink with fresh rhubarb juice and adding a dash of sparkling water to give some fizz. Four or five stalks of rhubarb will provide ⅓ cup (100ml) juice.

Tools: **Juicer (optional), mixing glass, barspoon/long spoon, tea strainer**

Glass: **Highball**

Ice: **Cubes**

Garnish: **Sweet cicely leaf and/or blood orange segment**

¼ cup (50ml) Roast Rhubarb Juice (see below)

⅔oz (20ml) Homemade Ginger Ale (see page 132) and ¼ cup (50ml) sparkling water or ¼ cup (50ml) freshly juiced raw rhubarb and ⅔oz (20ml) sparkling water

Squeeze of fresh lemon

Serves 1

Fill the mixing glass two-thirds of the way up with ice. Add the Roast Rhubarb Juice, ginger ale/fresh rhubarb juice (whichever you are using), and squeeze of lemon. Stir well to chill the drink properly. Strain into the serving glass, using a tea strainer to catch any bits, and top with the correct measure of sparkling water. Garnish with a sweet cicely leaf and/or a segment of blood orange.

ROAST RHUBARB JUICE

This recipe provides enough juice to make two mocktails.

4–5 stalks of rhubarb, cut into 1-in (2.5-cm) chunks

3 x 2-in (5-cm) pieces of orange peel

3 sprigs of sweet cicely leaves

1 finely chopped lemongrass stalk (outer layers removed)

5oz (150ml) blood orange juice (or regular orange juice if you prefer)

Small ovenproof skillet or frying pan
Fine-mesh strainer
Measuring pitcher

To roast the rhubarb, preheat the oven to 180°C/350°F/Gas 4. Put the rhubarb and other ingredients in the skillet or frying pan, and cover with the blood orange juice. Roast for about 40 minutes, stirring occasionally to prevent the rhubarb sticking or drying out. Remove from the oven, let cool, and strain ⅓ cup (100ml) of the juices into the pitcher, ready for making your mocktails.

Vegan and Virgin PIÑA COLADA

This really is a delicious mocktail to have morning, noon, or night. I am aware that coconuts have a high carbon footprint for me living in the U.K., but plenty of people enjoy a bounty of coconuts on their doorstep. Lucky them!

½ cup (100g) **organic young coconut meat (canned is fine)**

1 cup (250g) **frozen pineapple chunks**

2 tsp (10ml) **freshly squeezed lime juice**

1 tsp (5ml) **honey**

½ cup (125ml) **Coconut Milk Kefir (see page 128)**

Add all the ingredients (apart from the Coconut Milk Kefir) to the food blender and blend for 10 seconds on high. Add the Coconut Milk Kefir and blend on low for a further 5 seconds. Pop 3 ice cubes in the serving glass, pour in the mix, and garnish with a pineapple chunk and/or pineapple sage flower/leaf. Enjoy!

Tools: **Food blender**

Glass: **Highball/dessert**

Ice: **Cubes**

Garnish: **Pineapple chunk and/or pineapple weed (*Matricaria discoidea*) flower/leaf**

Serves 1

COCONUT WATER KEFIR
Strawberry Cosmo

The slightly fizzy, tart Coconut Water Kefir tastes delicious with strawberries (though you will find it mixes with endless combinations of juices or smoothies), and provides a level of complexity that will make your mocktails taste both grown-up and interesting.

1oz (30ml) Coconut Water Kefir (see page 127)
½ cup (65g) strawberries
1 cup (250ml) chilled sparkling water
Squeeze of fresh lime

Tools: **Food blender**
Glass: **Martini**
Ice: **Cubes**
Garnish: **Strawberry segment and basil sprig**

Serves 1

Put the Coconut Kefir Water and strawberries in the freezer for 30 minutes to chill, then place in the food blender and blend until smooth. Add the chilled sparkling water and a squeeze of lime, and pulse for a moment more. Pour the contents into the iced-filled Martini glass, and garnish with a segment of strawberry and a basil sprig.

STRAWBERRY AND LEMON VERBENA *Mocktail*

Using strawberries, lemon verbena (*Aloysia citrodora*) leaves, and sweet cicely (*Myrrhis odorata*) seeds, this mocktail really is a taste of summer—grown-up, herbaceous, and with enough sweetness for you to indulge yourself. Adding a splash of bitters, which contain a small amount of alcohol, is optional.

lemon verbena

5 ripe strawberries, washed and hulled

5 lemon verbena leaves

5 sweet cicely seeds

2 tsp (10ml) freshly squeezed lemon juice

Grind of coarse black pepper

4oz (120ml) sparkling water

2 dashes of Citrus Bitters (see page 75) or orange bitters (optional)

Tools: **Cocktail shaker with strainer, muddler, barspoon/mixing rod**

Glass: **Champagne/rocks/wine**

Ice: **Cubes**

Garnish: **Sweet cicely seeds and leaf, lemon verbena leaf**

Serves 1

Fill the serving glass with ice. Place the strawberries, lemon verbena leaves, and sweet cicely seeds in the bottom of the cocktail shaker and muddle thoroughly (see page 24) to release all the juices, essential oils, and flavors. Add the lemon juice and black pepper. Fill the shaker two-thirds of the way up with ice. Seal and shake hard for 20 seconds to really muddle things up and cool things down. Strain the mocktail into the serving glass. Top up with sparkling water, add the bitters (if using), and stir to combine. Garnish with sweet cicely seeds, if you wish, a sweet cicely leaf, and a lemon verbena leaf.

SEA BUCKTHORN AND FERMENTED BIRCH SAP
Mocktail

This mocktail is oozing zeitgeist health and coolness, but, in spite of itself, it's delicious! Sea buckthorn (*Hippophae rhamnoides*) is found growing everywhere, not just at the coast, so you can either make your own juice from wild berries or source it from reputable online suppliers. The berries are bursting with vitamin C, antioxidants, and omega oils, and are even high in protein. They have plenty of sourness, but none of the bitterness of citrus fruit. The naturally sweetened Fermented Birch Sap provides just the right amount of healthy sweetness to take the edge off, as well as adding more complexity and goodness.

1 cup (250ml) Fresh Sea Buckthorn Juice (see below) or store-bought sea buckthorn juice

1 cup (250ml) Fermented Birch Sap (see page 130)

Tools: **Mixing glass, barspoon/long spoon**

Glass: **Highball (x 4)**

Ice: **Cubes**

Garnish: **Flowering sprig of Darwin's barberry (*Berberis darwinii*)**

Serves 4 (makes approximately 1 pint/500ml)

Fill 4 highball glasses with ice. Pour 2oz (60ml) of sea buckthorn juice into each glass. Add the Fermented Birch Sap (about 2oz/60ml per serve) until it reaches the tops of the glasses, and stir. A cluster of Darwin's barberry flowers finishes the drink with an exquisite, tropical, sweet garnish.

FRESH SEA BUCKTHORN JUICE

The hellish thorns make harvesting sea buckthorn berries difficult. A good tip is to cut off whole branches covered in berries (you'll get about 12in/30cm of berries per branch) and freeze them, so you can just knock or shake the berries off and save yourself a world of pain and frustration. From four 12-in (30-cm) branches full of berries you will have enough juice to make four mocktails. Simply put the branches in a sealable container or plastic bag and keep them in the freezer for at least a couple of hours. Once the berries have frozen, knock or shake them into a large bowl and leave them to thaw fully. Use a potato masher to push or squeeze the juice out of the berries. Fine-strain the juice (see page 25) into a measuring pitcher, ready to make your mocktails.

LILAC AND NETTLE *Mocktail*

Lilac (*Syringa vulgaris*) is one of those heady, floral wonders that fills streets and parks with the unmistakeable scent of spring. To preserve as much of the flavor as possible, I have suggested something akin to a quick, cold-brewed tea. Young nettle (*Urtica dioica*) tips are bursting with detoxifying goodness and give drinks a wonderful tannic quality. Put the two together with a drop of honey and you've got yourself a gorgeous springtime sipper!

5oz (150ml) Lilac and Nettle Tea (see below)

Squeeze of fresh lemon

2 tsp (10ml) Honey Syrup (see page 16) or maple syrup

Tools: **Cocktail shaker with strainer**
Glass: **Rocks**
Ice: **Cubes**
Garnish: **Lilac blossoms**

Serves 1

Fill the rocks glass with ice and fill the cocktail shaker two-thirds of the way up with ice. Add the Lilac and Nettle Tea, squeeze of lemon, and your choice of syrup. Shake well and strain into the rocks glass. Garnish with lilac blossoms.

LILAC AND NETTLE TEA

This recipe provides enough tea to make five mocktails.

2 packed cups (about 4 handfuls) of lilac flowers (all greenery removed)

1 packed cup (about 2 handfuls) of young nettle leaves

3 cups (750ml) boiling water

Freshly squeezed juice of ½ lemon

1 tsp (5ml) Honey Syrup (see page 16) or maple syrup

Small nonreactive saucepan
Fine-mesh strainer
Measuring pitcher

Put the lilac flowers and nettle leaves in the nonreactive saucepan and add enough boiling water (about 3 cups/750ml) to cover the plant material. While the water is still hot, add the lemon juice and your choice of syrup, and stir. Allow the tea to cool naturally and leave for at least 2 hours and a maximum of 4 hours before straining into the pitcher, ready to make your mocktails.

Regal Mary
MOCKTAIL

If you have been experimenting with the ferments in *Chapter 6: Cultured Drinks*, try mixing some Beet Kvass with Water Kefir to make this virgin Bloody Mary. I advise not serving this mocktail over ice because this will water it down too much and make the kvass frothy when you shake it. Instead, "roll" the mocktail, which cools down the drink without the frothiness.

Tools: Measuring pitcher, barspoon/ wooden spoon, 2 mixing glasses, cocktail shaker with strainer

Glass: Collins

Ice: Cubes

Garnish: Lovage/celery/fennel stalk and nasturtium leaves and flower (if available)

1 cup (250ml) **Water Kefir (see page 126)**

2oz (60ml) **Beet Kvass (see page 125) or tomato juice**

1oz (30ml) **celery juice**

1 tsp (5ml) **freshly squeezed lemon juice**

Pinch of **sea salt**

Pinch of **black pepper**

Dash of **hot Tabasco**

2 dashes of **Bittermens Xocolatl Mole Bitters (optional)**

Serves 1

Add all the ingredients to the pitcher and stir. Fill one of the mixing glasses two-thirds of the way up with ice. Pour the mix into the mixing glass and immediately "roll" (or transfer) the whole mix, including the ice, into the other mixing glass. Repeat this process, back and forth between the two mixing glasses, until your drink is cold. Strain immediately into the Collins glass, garnish with a lovage/ celery/fennel stalk and nasturtium leaves and flowers, and serve.

Fruity and Flowery SUMMER MOCKTAIL

This delicious mocktail draws on the summery sweetness of red clover (*Trifolium pratense*) and meadowsweet (*Filipendula ulmaria*) flowers. As with a few of the mocktails in this section, I have suggested adding a dash of bitters, which contain a tiny amount of alcohol.

⅔oz (20ml) **Strawberry, Clover, and Meadowsweet Shrub (see page 84)**

⅓ cup (100ml) **sparkling water**

Dash of **Citrus Bitters (see page 75) or orange bitters (optional)**

Tools: **Barspoon/long spoon**
Glass: **Highball/rocks**
Ice: **Cubes**
Garnish: **Red clover blossom and meadowsweet buds**

Serves 1

Fill the highball or rocks glass with ice. Pour the Strawberry, Clover, and Meadowsweet Shrub into the glass. Top with the sparkling water and add a dash of your chosen bitters, if desired. Stir well and garnish with red clover blossom and meadowsweet buds.

COCKTAILS

From light aperitifs to heady woodland and seashore cocktails and fireside digestives, these cocktails should have you covered for all occasions and all habitats. Have fun mixing and matching whatever you have in season to create something truly fitting for the time and place. Enjoy!

DOUGLAS FIR GIN
and Bee Pollen Cocktail

This woodsy cocktail feels and tastes just right outdoors. In an ideal world, you would use pine pollen (see page 171) for the glass rim when making this cocktail. Pine pollen is difficult to find, however, so bee pollen makes a good alternative and is available all year round from reputable online suppliers. It provides a fantastic sweet rim for this drink. Opt for an expensive bee pollen from a supplier that uses sustainable methods to collect just enough pollen without damaging the health of the bee colony.

1oz (30ml) freshly squeezed lemon juice (for the rim)

1 tsp bee pollen (for the rim)

2oz (60ml) Douglas Fir-infused Gin (see page 54)

¾oz (22ml) Wild Dry Vermouth (see page 55)

Tools: **2 saucers, mixing glass, barspoon/long spoon, strainer**
Glass: **Martini/sherry**
Ice: **Cubes**
Garnish: **Douglas fir (*Pseudotsuga menziesii*) sprig**

Serves 1

Pour the lemon juice into the saucer. Put the bee pollen in the other saucer. Dip the outside rim of the Martini/sherry glass in the lemon juice and turn it to cover half the glass. Coat the lemon juice with the bee pollen and brush off any excess.

Fill the mixing glass two-thirds of the way up with ice. Pour the Douglas Fir-infused Gin and Wild Dry Vermouth into the glass and stir for 20 seconds to cool down and dilute the drink sufficiently. Strain the cocktail into the serving glass. Garnish with a sprig of Douglas fir.

Bee pollen is the food of young bees. It is approximately 40 percent protein and considered one of nature's most completely nourishing foods, containing nearly all the nutrients required by humans.

BASIL-INFUSED

Dolin Blanc Spritz

This is a beautiful, herbaceous, low-alcohol aperitif. We are lucky at Midnight Apothecary to be close to a wonderful, small-batch soda company called Square Root Soda, who started in the same year as us. They make exquisite tonic waters and sodas, and we like to pair our Basil-infused Dolin Blanc Vermouth with their Artemesia Tonic, a delicious blend of wormwood, mugwort, and tarragon. Most of you are out of reach of this beauty, so my advice—if you're not making your own tonic water—is to find a similar small-batch company. That said, I'm pretty pleased with my tonic water, so, if you have the time, you will love using it in this.

2oz (60ml) Basil-infused Dolin Blanc
Vermouth (see page 60)
¾oz (22ml) Homemade Tonic
Water Syrup (see page 78) and 3oz
(90ml) sparkling water (or just use
about 4oz/120ml ready-diluted
commercial tonic water)
Dash of Citrus Bitters (see page 75)
or orange bitters

Put a handful of ice cubes in the large Champagne or wine glass. Pour the Basil-infused Dolin Blanc Vermouth and the combined Homemade Tonic Water Syrup and sparkling water (or store-bought tonic water) over the ice cubes. Add a dash of bitters, stir, and serve, garnished with a basil sprig.

Tools: **Long spoon/drinking straw**
Glass: **Large Champagne/wine**
Ice: **Cubes**
Garnish: **Basil sprig**
Serves 1

Wild NEGRONI

The combination of bitter and sweet tastes creates an irresistible aperitif and is still one of my favorites to put the world to rights. It's a great way to show off your homemade Wild Dry Vermouth but, of course, there are lots of excellent commercial varieties available. Campari, while very bitter, is also on the sweet side, so I prefer to accompany it with a dry vermouth. The gin is up to you. We use our beloved local Jensen's Bermondsey Dry in this cocktail and sometimes use it infused with fennel seed to give the drink more herbaceous notes—again, it's entirely up to you. The key is to serve this cocktail ice-cold, but not too diluted with ice, so make sure you use the biggest ice cubes you can find in order to delay the melting time.

1oz (30ml) **Wild Dry Vermouth (see page 55)**

1oz (30ml) **Campari**

1oz (30ml) **dry gin, such as Jensen's Bermondsey Dry**

Tools: **Mixing glass, barspoon/long spoon, strainer**

Glass: **Rocks**

Ice: **Large or regular cubes**

Garnish: **Blood orange wheel, plus a flowering sprig of rosemary, anise hyssop (*Agastache foeniculum*), or hyssop (*Hyssopus officinalis*), and a strip of orange zest**

Fill the rocks glass with one large ice cube or about four regular ones. Fill the mixing glass two-thirds of the way up with ice. Pour all the ingredients over the ice and stir for at least 20 seconds to really cool the drink down—you want to see condensation on the outside of the mixing glass. Strain the cocktail into the rocks glass. Garnish with the blood orange wheel and a flowering sprig of your choice. Rub the outside of the orange zest around the rim of the glass and then squeeze it into the drink to release the gorgeous essential oils. Plop the zest into the glass and enjoy!

Serves 1

Wild Vermouth
AND FERMENTED BIRCH SAP COCKTAIL

This cocktail provides another way of lengthening and enjoying some Wild Dry Vermouth, while getting the health benefits of Fermented Birch Sap. It also plays around with woodland flavors, making it the perfect cocktail to enjoy outdoors.

2oz (60ml) Wild Dry Vermouth (see page 55)

3oz (90ml) Fermented Birch Sap (see page 130)

Simply fill the rocks glass with ice. Pour the Wild Dry Vermouth over the ice and top up with the Fermented Birch Sap. Garnish with some sweet woodruff and enjoy!

Tools: **Barspoon/longspoon**

Glass: **Rocks**

Ice: **Cubes**

Garnish: **Sweet woodruff (*Galium odoratum*)**

Serves 1

sweet woodruff

The ROCKPOOL

This cocktail conjures up the essence of the beach. We have umami seaweed with the moisture-giving ice plant (*Carpobrotus edulis*), earthy wild fennel (*Foeniculum vulgare*), oyster plant (*Mertensia maritima*), which does taste of oysters, and citrusy French sorrel (*Rumex scutatus*). The dry vermouth adds a touch of sweetness to round everything out, while the drop of salt makes all the flavors pop. I've used pepper dulse (*Osmundea pinnatifida*), but you can play around with other fresh seaweeds or just use store-bought dried seaweed. The idea is to make this cocktail instantly on the beach, albeit with a bit of equipment! To get maximum flavor from the herbs, I juice them at home and take them to the beach. Or, if you're at the beach and have just picked the herbs, you can quickly infuse their flavors into a liquid using a professional cream whipper and N2O (nitrous oxide) cartridges (see page 21)—not an everyday item for your beach bag, but this equipment is worth it if you want instant infusions on your foraging forays. If you don't want the hassle, the cocktail is drinkable without the juiced/infused herbs.

8 small pepper dulse fronds (two per serving)

1 cup (250ml) vodka (if using a professional cream whipper, you'll need an extra 1 cup/250ml)

1⅓oz (40ml) dry vermouth

1⅓oz (40ml) juiced ice plant, French sorrel, oyster plant, and wild fennel (juice according to the manufacturer's instructions) or a small handful of each herb (optional)

Dried seaweed and sea salt, for the glass rim (optional)

Tools: **Sterilized sealable glass jar (as used for jellies and jams), professional cream whipper with 2 N2O cartridges (if you haven't brought freshly juiced herbs), measuring pitcher, mixing glass, barspoon/long spoon, saucer (optional), hawthorne strainer, tea strainer**
Glass: **Martini (x 4)**
Ice: **Cubes**
Garnish: **Dulse frond**

Serves 4

Place the pepper dulse fronds in the jar and pour in 1 cup (250ml) of vodka. Seal the jar and infuse for 15 minutes. Remove the fronds. Put some ice cubes in each Martini glass to chill them thoroughly while you prepare the cocktails.

If you haven't brought ready-juiced herbs, roughly tear and smack some freshly picked herbs in your hand, place them in the cream whipper, and pour in another 1 cup (250ml) of vodka. Charge the whipper with the N2O cartridges (see page 21), following the manufacturer's instructions, and vent.

To build your cocktails two at a time, fill the mixing glass two-thirds of the way up with ice. Add 4oz (125ml) of the seaweed-infused vodka, ⅔oz (20ml) of the dry vermouth, and ⅔oz (20ml) of the juiced herbs. (If you are using the cream-whipper method, add ⅔oz/20ml of the infused herb vodka to the mix and use slightly less seaweed-infused vodka.) Stir the

ingredients thoroughly to really chill down and dilute the drink. Discard the ice cubes from the Martini glasses.

To add a salty rim, dip the outer rim of the Martini glasses in water and then roll them in a mix of dried seaweed and sea salt sprinkled onto a saucer. Double-strain (see page 25) the cocktail into each glass. Repeat for the other two glasses. Garnish each cocktail with a dulse frond, then sit back, watch the sunset, and enjoy.

seashore herbs

It was forager Mark Williams (see *Featured Foragers*, on page 166) who introduced me to the exquistie variety of seaweed called pepper dulse (*Osmundea pinnatifida*). He explained to me that it is called the "truffle of the sea" because of its extraordinarily gorgeous, mushroom-y, peppery, lobster-y taste. It's not to be confused with ordinary dulse (*Palmaria palmata*), which, although far more common, does not quite compare. However, even ordinary dulse will give nutty, licorice, smoky notes to your drink.

SHERRY AND AQUAFABA
Aperitif

Aquafaba is the name of the viscous liquid you get after boiling bagged pulses such as beans and chickpeas (garbanzo beans). The same liquid is also found in canned versions of these foods. In 2014 the French chef Joel Roessel discovered that it can be used as a replacement for egg white and, of course, the vegan cocktail crowd gave a loud cheer. Now everyone can enjoy foam on their cocktails. This really does make a delicious aperitif. Essentially, I've taken the famous sherry Flip, which is traditionally made with a whole egg white, and used chickpea water instead. The cocktail is sweetened slightly with yacón syrup (although you can use whichever sweetener you like). The sherry is mushroom-infused, so this provides the ideal pick-me-up, go-to brunch drink!

2oz (60ml) Porcini-infused Amontillado Sherry (see page 62)

1oz (30ml) canned chickpea water (i.e. aquafaba)

2 tsp (10ml) yacón syrup

Tools: **Cocktail shaker with strainer**

Glass: **Sherry**

Ice: **Cubes**

Garnish: **Fennel fronds and scented geranium (*Pelargonium*) leaf**

Serves 1

Fill the cocktail shaker two-thirds of the way up with ice. Add the Porcini-infused Amontillado Sherry, chickpea water, and yacón syrup. If you have a spare metal spiral from a hawthorne strainer, add this to the shaker because it reduces the amount of shaking time needed to get the desired emulsifying effect from the chickpea water. Otherwise, just shake harder and for longer. Shake for at least 20 seconds. Strain the cocktail into the sherry glass and garnish with whatever herbaceous wonders you have at hand. Here, I've used fennel fronds and a scented geranium leaf.

LIQUORE
Digestif

The Cherry and Cacao Liquore really is too strong to drink on its own. However, if you water it down with a couple of ice cubes and a drop of water, you have yourself a rather special digestif.

2oz (60ml) Cherry and Cacao Liquore (see page 90)
1oz (30ml) water

Tools: **Mixing glass, barspoon/long spoon, strainer**
Glass: **Sherry**
Ice: **Cubes**
Garnish: **Pair of cherries**

Serves 1

Fill a mixing glass with a handful of ice. Pour the Cherry and Cacao Liquore and water over the ice and stir for about 10 seconds. Strain the cocktail into the sherry glass and garnish with a pair of cherries.

Gorse and Cherry Blossom GIMLET

This springtime outdoor sipper with a kick is perfect for a picnic. You can prepare and bottle it in advance and then just bring ice to cool it down. It's best enjoyed by the coast or on heath or moorland, with the coconut-y waft of gorse in the air, or under a cherry blossom tree surrounded by the almond-y scents of confetti-like petals.

Tools: Cocktail shaker with strainer
Glass: Martini/coupe
Ice: Cubes
Garnish: Gorse (*Ulex europaeus*) flower and/or cherry blossom

2oz (60ml) Gorse Rum (see page 63)
½oz (15ml) Cherry Blossom and Flowering Currant Cordial (see page 70)
½oz (15ml) freshly squeezed lime juice

Fill the cocktail shaker two-thirds of the way up with ice. Add all the ingredients, cover, shake, and strain into the cocktail glass. Garnish with a gorse flower and/or cherry blossom.

Serves 1

Quince DELIGHT

This cocktail exudes an almost rose-like, autumnal perfume and, frankly, I like it neat, stirred over ice, and then strained into a Martini glass. However, here I added the tiniest smidge of earthy carameliness by using a dash of maple syrup.

2oz (60ml) Quince Vodka with Szechuan Pepper, Star Anise, and Juniper Berries (see page 52)
1 tsp (5ml) Grade B (Grade A dark robust) maple syrup
3 drops of Becky's Pear, Quince, and Apple Windfall Bitters (see page 77)

Tools: **Mixing glass, barspoon/long spoon, hawthorne strainer**
Glass: **Martini**
Ice: **Cubes**
Garnish: **Quince slice, peeled and dehydrated (or dry-roasted)**

Serves 1

Simply stir the three ingredients in a mixing glass filled with plenty of ice cubes to cool the drink thoroughly. Strain the mix into the Martini glass. Balance the quince slice on the side of the glass.

VARIATION

To lengthen the Quince Delight cocktail, fill a highball or rocks glass with ice and top up with some organic pear juice and a drop of soda water.

SPOOKY COW
and Tonic

During the fall (autumn) and winter, the bar at Midnight Apothecary cozies up with special weekly themed nights, including the Hallowe'en Spooktacular at the end of October and the Bonfire Night Special the following week. We often serve the Bonfire of the Vani-Teas cocktail (see page 105) on Bonfire Night. People are drawn to the enticing fire pit, to ward off the cold and any unwelcome spirits. We create a spider-web forest and, aside from the usual sizzling-hot food and marshmallows, we go to town on the themed cocktails. This spooky cocktail is full of good spirits to ward off the nasty ones and prepare you for the cold nights ahead. If you've ever encountered a pineberry, you'll know it's crying out to be paired with a couple of redcurrants and turned into a zombie! This is a delicious, strong, aromatic drink, with just enough sweetness in the angostura bitters to balance things out.

Tools: **Mixing glass, barspoon/long spoon, hawthorne strainer**

Glass: **Rocks**

Ice: **Cubes**

Garnish: **Fennel seed/pollen head, 1 pineberry, 2 redcurrants, 2 toothpicks (cocktail sticks)**

2oz (60ml) Fennel Seed Vodka (see page 51) or other smooth vodka

3 generous dashes of angostura bitters

Small squeeze of fresh lemon

Tonic water (to taste)

Serves 1

Fill the mixing glass with ice and add the fennel-infused vodka, angostura bitters, and a small squeeze of lemon. Stir and then strain into the ice-filled rocks glass. Add tonic water to taste. Add the fennel seed/pollen head and "zombie" garnish. Make the "zombie" by threading the pineberry onto two toothpicks (cocktail sticks) and adding the two redcurrants for eyes.

HOT STRAWBERRY *Fizz*

The heat of this delicious summer sipper comes from the Szechuan peppercorns.

4 strawberries
¼ tsp Szechuan peppercorns
1½oz (45ml) Old Tom gin
(I use Jensen's)
½ tsp (2.5ml) raw honey
Pinch of sea salt
4oz (120ml) Ginger, Lemon, and Lavender Kombucha (see page 124)

Tools: **Cocktail shaker with strainer, muddler**
Glass: **Highball**
Ice: **Cubes**
Garnish: **Strawberry, lavender sprig, and fresh Szechuan peppercorn sprig (optional)**

Serves 1

Fill the highball glass with ice. Add the strawberries and peppercorns to the cocktail shaker. Muddle (see page 24) to crush both ingredients. Add the gin, honey, and salt, and fill the shaker two-thirds of the way up with ice. Cover, shake for 20 seconds, and then strain into the highball glass. Top up with the Ginger, Lemon, and Lavender Kombucha. Garnish with a strawberry, if you wish, and a sprig of lavender (and also a Szechuan peppercorn sprig, if you have one).

FRUITY KOMBUCHA COCKTAIL

I am putting this recipe here for no other reason than to demonstrate the versatility of kombucha when mixing drinks. If you have made a batch of Simple Kombucha (see page 122), you can add lots of fruits at the second-ferment stage. For example, try adding ½ cup (65g) of raspberries or blueberries (slightly muddled first to release their juices, see page 24) to the initial kombucha. The resulting combination creates a great cocktail when mixed with a shot of rum, a squeeze of fresh lime, and perhaps a tiny drop of honey to sweeten. Serve this cocktail over ice.

Toasted Kumquat
AND AMARETTO SOUR

This cocktail tastes of Christmas to me. It's a seasonal indulgence with the almond-y sweetness of amaretto, but is kicked into touch with the whiskey and calmed by the warming, soothing, spicy Kumquat, Thyme, Cinnamon, and Honey Syrup.

1oz (30ml) whisky

½oz (15ml) amaretto

½oz (15ml) Kumquat, Thyme, Cinnamon, and Honey Syrup (see page 72)

¾oz (22ml) freshly squeezed lemon juice

1 egg white or 1oz (30ml) canned chickpea water (see page 158)

1 thyme sprig

Tools: **Cocktail shaker with strainer, tea strainer**

Glass: **Martini**

Ice: **Cubes**

Garnish: **½ grilled kumquat and thyme sprig, toothpick (cocktail stick)**

Serves 1

Create the garnish first by grilling half a kumquat over a gas flame on your stovetop, under a broiler (grill), over a campfire, or with a culinary blowtorch. The smell will set you up for Christmas! Put the kumquat half on a toothpick (cocktail stick) and wrap with the sprig of thyme. Set aside.

Fill a cocktail shaker two-thirds of the way up with ice. Smack another sprig of thyme between your palms to release the essential oils and drop it into the cocktail shaker. Add the whisky, amaretto, Kumquat, Thyme, Cinnamon, and Honey Syrup, lemon juice, and egg white/chickpea water to the shaker. If you have a spare metal spiral from a hawthorn strainer, add this to the shaker to help emulsify the egg white/chickpea water while shaking. Seal and shake

for at least 20 seconds until you have a really good foam. Use the tea strainer to double-strain (see page 25) the cocktail and make sure you catch all the little pieces of thyme. Garnish with the grilled kumquat and the sprig of thyme.

FEATURED FORAGERS: LIZ KNIGHT AND MARK WILLIAMS

I met Liz Knight of Forage Fine Foods, in Herefordshire, U.K., at one of her wild food-tasting sessions and was wowed by her plant knowledge, sense of smell and taste, and ability to combine exquisite foraged flavors in jellies, syrups, rubs, and salts. Liz lives on a farm in the Welsh borders with her husband and three children. I'd read her descriptions of the reality of this bucolic-sounding existence and everything she did and wrote made me want to get to know her more.

Liz runs various courses from her farm and has teamed up with Mark Williams of Galloway Wild Foods, in Scotland. Mark is a prominent foraging teacher, guide, and fungi expert, with over 25 years' experience. Liz invited me to attend their joint course. Together, they took us through the fields, hedgerows, and woods. With eyes permanently cast downward, Liz was keen to pick Mark's brains regarding the huge variety of mushrooms, while Mark offered Liz things to taste to find out how she might use them.

Both Liz and Mark were passionate about passing on their knowledge of the flavors and uses of the finds, such as the dried seedheads of what they called their "native spice rack," in the form of hogweed and angelica seeds. However, what came across most was a broader excitement about the plants and fungi's connection to the land—not just for our culinary needs, but also for the health of our bodies and the soil. I learnt such a huge amount from them.

Aside from their encyclopedic plant knowledge, I was also humbled by their approach to foraging and mixing. Unlike at the Midnight Apothecary, where I carefully infuse, measure, pour, and balance, to ensure each specific drink tastes the same, their approach was the complete opposite. They were more inclined to rustle up some instant wild vermouth with a bit of this and that, or pour gin through a scrunched-up bunch of cleavers (*Galium aparine*) to get a decent flavor. For them, it was more important for those on the course to pick herbs, berries, seeds, leaves, and roots, stick them in a professional cream whipper (see page 21), and get an instant taste of the foraged flavors around them.

Mark's collaborations with serious chefs in Scotland have developed his fermenting and pickling techniques. I sampled an incredible array of his prize potions, many of which had been lovingly prepared over months. So, it wasn't all instant wild drinking! Liz is also no stranger to wild drinks. Her cocktails are some of the most original I've encountered and have flavors that I can't top. Her shelves are bulging with tinctures, vinegars, syrups, and infusions that both surprise and delight. Together Liz and Mark shared their ideas in ego-less excitement. Liz has kindly provided a delicious tonic recipe for this book.

Liz's WILD TONICS

As Liz explains, "Winter foragers with lurgies reach for immune-boosting wild tonics to chase away their ills." Fortunately, wild tonics are best administered with medicinal gin in a cocktail glass. These wild tonics are gathered from summer onward and make delicious use of "wild aspirin"—meadowsweet (*Filipendula ulmaria*)—and immune-boosting elderberries, antioxidant-rich rosehips, hawberries (the berries from hawthorn/*Crataegus monogyna*), and blackberries. These are all boosted with the herbal cure-alls of nettle (*Urtium dioica*), cleaver (*Galium aparine*), and dandelion (*Taraxacum officinale*) leaves.

hawberries

TONIC SYRUP

3½oz (100g) each of rosehips, hawberries, blackberries, and elderberries (plus mulberries, if you have them)
Honey (see Method for quantity)
Handful of young nettle, cleaver, and dandelion leaves
2 tsp dried meadowsweet flowers

Saucepan
Flexible scraper
Fine sieve
Measuring pitcher
Sealable presentation bottle(s), sterilized (see page 24)

Makes approximately 1 pint (500ml)

Everyone knows you need a little sugar (or honey) to help the medicine go down. But there is a lot of medicine here and not much honey. This recipe provides enough syrup for approximately 15 drinks.

Add the rosehips and hawberries to the saucepan. Cover with water and cook until soft. Then add the blackberries and elderberries (and the mulberries, if using). Simmer until cooked, then use the flexible scraper to press the juices through the sieve into the pitcher. Retain the pulp, as you'll need this to make the Tonicy Gin (see page 169).

Pour the juice into the pan, then, for every 3½oz (100ml) of liquid, dissolve 2oz (60ml) of honey. Bring the sweet juice to a simmer until all the honey has dissolved.

Let cool slightly (so the liquid is not boiling) and then stir in a handful of young nettle, cleaver, and dandelion leaves, as well as the dried meadowsweet flowers. Leave to infuse for about 1 hour before straining and funneling into the sterilized presentation bottle(s). Keep the syrup in the refrigerator for up to 1 month or freeze until needed.

TONICY GIN

Berry/hip pulp and strained leaves (retained from a batch of Tonic Syrup, see page 167)
700 or 750ml bottle of gin

1-quart (1-liter) wide-mouthed, sealable jar, sterilized (see page 24)
Sealable presentation bottle(s), sterilized (see page 24)

Makes approximately 1½ pints (750ml)

Waste not, want not—and what a delicious way in which to imbibe your tonicy pulp!

Add the pulp and strained leaves left over from making a batch of Tonic Syrup to the sterilized jar and cover with gin. Seal and leave for a few days before straining into the sterilized presentation bottle(s). Store in a cool, dark place and consume within 6 months.

nettle

WILD GIN AND TONIC

1oz (30ml) Tonic Syrup (see page 167)
1oz (30ml) Tonicy Gin (see above)
3oz (90ml) sour apple juice or apple verjuice

Tools: **Mixing glass, barspoon/ long spoon, strainer**
Glass: **Highball**
Ice: **Cubes**
Garnish: **String of nettle (*Urtica dioica*) seeds (nature's caffeine)**

Serves 1

This is a two-part affair; choose according to your affliction. Once your first sneeze hits, reach for your Tonic Syrup, Tonicy Gin, and some sour apple juice or apple verjuice— and ease your aches with a Wild Gin and Tonic. Perfect for cooling a fevered brow.

Fill the highball glass with ice. Mix the Tonic Syrup and Tonicy Gin with the sour apple juice or apple verjuice in the mixing glass. Strain the cocktail into the highball glass and garnish with a string of nature's caffeine— some nettle seeds to nibble on.

If you've got a chill, simply heat the apple juice or a dry cider, and add the wild elixirs to your steaming cup. Serve under a feather duvet and sip away your wild woes...

VARIATION

For a non-alcoholic version of Wild Gin and Tonic, simply replace the 1oz (30ml) of Tonicy Gin with the same quantity of apple verjuice or sour apple juice.

Into THE WOODS

In a bid to dial down the sweetness, I've maximized the essence of smoke, nuts, mushrooms, and pine that I associate with a walk in the woods. You don't need to include all the botanicals or techniques here, but I wanted to demonstrate the range of ideas you can experiment with to extract as much flavor, texture, and scent from one habitat: a woodland. The amontillado sherry brings its own nutty, oaky sweetness, as does the pine pollen in the optional savory rim, while the drops of hazelnut oil provide a lightly viscous mouth-feel and nutty, sweet, and herbal aroma. The Citrus Bitters bring acid and sugar to the party—in a tiny dose, but just enough to balance everything out.

2oz (60ml) Oaked Vodka (see page 48) or unoaked vodka

2 tsp (10ml) Porcini-infused Amontillado Sherry (see page 62)

3 drops of Citrus Bitters (see page 75)

3 drops of Sage-infused Hazelnut Oil (see page 86)

Tools: **Saucer (optional), mixing glass, stirring rod/long spoon, hawthorne strainer, dropper/pipette**

Glass: **Sherry**

Ice: **Cubes**

Garnish: **¾oz (22ml) freshly squeezed lemon juice or pine resin, plus Dried Porcini Mushroom and Pine Pollen Mix (optional, see right)**

Serves 1

This cocktails starts with the optional garnish. Dip the sherry glass in a saucer of lemon juice or resin and then turn the outside edge of the glass in the Dried Porcini Mushroom and Pine Pollen Mix, to coat one half of the rim.

Fill the mixing glass two-thirds of the way up with ice. Add all the ingredients (except the oil). Stir for at least 30 seconds, or until condensation appears on the outside of the glass. Slide the hawthorne strainer over the mixing glass and strain the contents into the sherry glass. Use the dropper/pipette to place 3 drops of the oil on the surface of the cocktail.

VARIATION

If you don't want to go to make Oaked Vodka (see page 48), you can just use unoaked vodka instead. Alternatively, use 1½oz (45ml) of the Douglas Fir-infused Gin (see page 54) and add ½oz (15ml) of a smoky Scotch such as Laphroaig. Then continue with the remaining ingredients and method, as for the main recipe.

DRIED PORCINI MUSHROOM AND PINE POLLEN MIX

To make a savory mix to decorate the rim of the glass, grind a few dried porcini mushrooms into a powder using a pestle and mortar or coffee grinder, and add some pine pollen. Store the mix in an airtight container for a few weeks.

Pine pollen has some interesting properties. It can raise your testosterone levels slightly and may also balance your androgen and estrogen levels! Pine pollen is also packed with anti-inflammatory properties and reduces your sensitivity to pain. If you happen to brush past a pine tree that emanates a yellow mist when you touch it, then you are in a pine pollen cloud, so feel free to knock some into your glass.

RESOURCES

BOOKS

The Forager Handbook by Miles Irving, Ebury Press, 2009 A guide to the edible plants of Great Britain.

Food For Free by Richard Mabey, Collins 1972 This is still the classic go-to reference book and has been revised with color photographs and turned into a Collins Gem pocket guide so that you can take it foraging.

Edible Wild Plants: A North American Field Guide by Thomas Elias and Peter Dykeman, Sterling, 1990 A very useful book for a wild food library because it provides 1–4 color photographs of each of the 220 wild plants it identifies, together with a range map and guide to each plant's uses.

Field Guide to Edible Wild Plants: Eastern and Central North America by Lee Allen Peterson, Peterson Field Guide Series No 23, 1999 Usefully, this guide includes shrubs, trees, vines, and non-showy flowering plants that you might not find in a regular wildflower guide.

Jekka's Complete Herb Book by Jekka McVicar, Kyle Cathie, 2009 This is my go-to book for anyone who loves gardening and cooking. It has everything from planting plans, beautiful photography, tips on how to propagate, grow, prune, and harvest a huge selection of herbs to a wealth of information on their culinary and medicinal applications.

Ferment, Pickle, Dry: Ancient Methods, Modern Meals by Simon Poffley and Gaba Smolinska-Poffley, Frances Lincoln, 2016 Co-written by Simon from The Fermentarium, this is packed with amazing recipes and beautiful photography by Kim Lightbody.

The Art of Fermentation: An In-depth Exploration of Essential Concepts and Processes from Around the World by Sandor Ellix Katz, Chelsea Green Publishing, 2012 Widely regarded as a classic in food literature; it does what it says beautifully.

WEBSITES

www.eatweeds.co.uk Robin Harford's Wild Food Guide to the edible plants of Britain. A fantastic resource, with plenty of information on courses and recipes, too.

www.gallowaywildfoods.com Mark Williams' site is absolutely jam-packed with wonderful tips, recipes, and knowledge about wild food and drink and he is very generous in sharing knowledge from other websites and blogs around the world. Also provides great foraging trips in Scotland.

www.capitalgrowth.org Supporter of Midnight Apothecary when we needed some good topsoil and bursting with practical advice and support for food-growing communities in London.

www.thelondonorchardproject. org Another wonderful provider of information and support to encourage Londoners to plant, care for, and harvest fruit trees across the capital.

www.notfarfromthetree.org A Toronto-based project based around picking fruit and distributing it by bike around Toronto.

www.cityfruit.org Another community-based fruit project in Seattle that maps existing trees and teaches people how to care for and maximize their harvests.

TWITTER ACCOUNTS

@KnowWildFood Canadian Dylan Gordon posts interesting tweets on the Canadian wild food industry and foraging in general.

@ReneRedzepiNoma Gourmet forager and founder of Noma—still tweeting inspiring dishes and wild ingredients from around the world

@SummerStarCoop A U.S. forager/farmer perspective.

@markwildfood Mark Williams of www.gallowaywildfoods.com tweets updates of his incredible wild food and drink forays—very entertaining.

@foragefinefoods Liz Knight manages to be informative and entertaining while balancing childcare (literally) as she works.

@Jonthepoacher What Jonathan Cook doesn't know about wild edibles on Walthamstow Marshes isn't worth knowing! Very helpful guide and mentor.

EDIBLE FLOWERS

www.maddocksfarmorganics. co.uk Huge variety of organic edible flowers grown by Jan Billington in south Devon, England.

www.themodernsaladgrower.co.uk Cornwall-based Sean O'Neill grows an abundance of unusual and wild ingredients for your cocktail treats and sells them online in the U.K.

COCKTAIL COURSES

www.thecocktailgardener.co.uk Cheeky plug for my website! I run courses and masterclasses from time to time, so check out the website or contact me if you would like something bespoke.

FORAGED FOOD AND INGREDIENTS

www.foragefinefoods.com Exquisite small-batch syrups, spice blends, and rubs made by Liz Knight in Herefordshire, England.

www.forager.org.uk U.K. supplier of wild plants, fungi, and syrups.

www.cornishseaweed.co.uk Sustainably free-dived, organic Cornish seaweeds available online.

FORAGING COURSES AND EXPERTS IN THE U.K.

www.gallowaywildfoods.com Back to Mark Williams again (see Websites, opposite), who runs courses in Scotland and Wales that are guaranteed to be informative, enjoyable, and delicious!

www.foragefinefoods.com Forager and potion-maker extraordinaire (see Foraged Food and Ingredients) also runs foraging courses and feasts... not to be missed if you get the chance.

www.theherbalhub.com Herbalist, forager, and natural cosmetics maker Vivienne Campbell runs amazing online courses so, although she is based on the west coast of Ireland, you can join her wonderfully informative network and take part in her courses wherever you are in the world.

www.foragelondon.co.uk John Rensten, forager and blogger, who leads foraging walks in and around London.

www.coastalsurvival.com In addition to running bushcraft courses, Fraser Christian is a fully qualified chef and professional forager who runs wonderful foraging courses in the U.K.

www.fathen.org A wild cookery school in west Cornwall, run by botanist and chef Caroline Davey. Caroline will take you for beautiful foraging forays and teach you how to identify and cook your treasures to perfection.

HERBS AND ESSENTIAL OILS
(Catering grade)

www.jekkasherbfarm.com Jekka's herbetum, near Bristol, displays the largest collection of culinary herbs in the U.K. and opens its doors several times a year for open days and masterclasses. Her blog is also well worth following.

www.baldwins.co.uk Purveyors of dried herbs and spices since 1844, fantastic apothecary bottles, and great bittering agents, particularly bark and wormwood. Based in London.

www.wildharvestuk.com U.K. suppliers to the catering trade of unusual herbs, edible flowers, and edible-flower extracts (e.g. jasmine).

www.tenzingmomo.com The West Coast's oldest and largest herbal apothecary and perfumery based in Seattle with an online store.

www.mountainroseherbs.com U.S. supplier of organic herbs (including ethically wild-harvested and Kosher-certified botanical products), spices, loose-leaf teas, essential oils, and herbal extracts.

www.dandelionbotanical.com U.S. natural apothecary based in Seattle that supplies certified organic herbs, spices, and botanicals.

www.oliveology.co.uk The finest Greek herbs, oils, and honey based in Borough Market, London, with an online store.

FERMENTATION EQUIPMENT AND COURSES

www.thefermentarium.org.uk Wonderful courses on fermentation of all kinds based in Walthamstow, east London (and big thank you for providing me with milk kefir grains!).

LIQUEURS

www.devondistillery.com An artisan distiller in south Devon with a passion for Italian Grappa and an award-winning product—the unique Dappa.

www.ciderbrandy.co.uk The Somerset Cider Brandy Company based in Somerset, U.K., makes cider, cider brandy, apple eau-de-vie, and morello cherries in eau-de-vie.

www.mothersruin.net Forager and proprietor of Walthamstow's Mother's Ruin Gin Palace in east London, Becky Wynn Griffiths (see Featured Forager, page 76) makes a range of unique and award-winning liqueurs.

SMALL BATCH AND RARE LIQUOR

www.gerrys.uk.com Gerry's Wines and Spirits is based in the heart of Soho, London. If you can't find what you're looking for anywhere else, they are bound to have it!

OTHER BOOZE

www.bermondseygin.com Bermondsey distillers, just round the corner from Midnight Apothecary, of the superb Old Tom gin made to an unsweetened 1840s' recipe and a lovely Bermondsey Dry.

www.hiverbeers.com Makers of Hiver, The Honey Beer, a beautifully delicate and floral beer using rural and urban honey. Based in Bermondsey, south-east London, and regular supporters of Midnight Apothecary.

www.squarerootsoda.co.uk Makers of delicious small-batch sodas and tonic waters in Hackney, London. Seasonal additions constantly included.

MIXOLOGY AND GOURMET CATERING EQUIPMENT

www.cocktailkingdom.com Online suppliers of every conceivable piece of bar equipment you might need, from shakers to julep cups to dashers, bitters, and books.

www.modernistpantry.com Website supplying flavor pearls and a wide range of mixology kits/chemicals to make your own, as well as professional cream whippers.

www.nisbets.co.uk Huge selection of catering and bar equipment.

www.ebay.com A wide range of vintage and collectable bar tools, equipment, and glasses.

MISCELLANEOUS

www.instagram.com/pan_ldn Sensational seasonal Greek cooking from herb-centered Despina Siahuli. Pan London is her labor of love—using the finest local and seasonal ingredients to reinvent the Greek dishes of her heritage. Serves up exquisite fare weekly at Midnight Apothecary and runs gatherings and workshops around London.

INDEX

PICTURE CREDITS

All photography by Kim Lightbody,
except for:
p.23 Gavin Kingcome
p.24 William Lingwood
p.51 Pete Cassidy
pp.120–121 Toby Scott
p.131 Ryan Paul

ACKNOWLEDGMENTS

A huge thank you to Kim Lightbody, photographer and now friend whose
talent and humor have again made the adventure fun and the book beautiful.
To foragers Becky Wynn-Griffiths, Liz West, and Mark Williams, and gardener
extraordinaire Jekka McVicar for their inspiring knowledge, generosity, and
enthusiasm. To Caroline West for brilliant editing and painless cajoling. To
Cathy, Catherine, Donna, and Janet for their gardening skills and for regularly
channeling their artistry to turn Midnight Apothecary into an enchanted forest
or spooky chamber at very short notice. To the Brunel Museum for allowing us
to blossom as a venture. To Anita McNaught for allowing me to take over her
herb garden in the Ashdown Forest for future foodie and foraging adventures.
To the guests at Midnight Apothecary who continue to bring their enthusiasm
and sense of adventure to the bar. And to the brilliant bar crew who continue
to make Midnight Apothecary an hilarious place to work: Jack, Claire, Heather,
Ella, Alice, Fred, Donna, Lewis, Gavin, Lizzie, Tim, Ben, and Dan. Finally, to my
precious brother David and niece Ruby for their love and support.